UNLEASH THE
NEURONS

Design Thinking

I0490977

MANOJ KUMAR PATEL
KSHYUDHA S. CHOUDHURY

INDIA · SINGAPORE · MALAYSIA

Notion Press

No. 8, 3rd Cross Street,
CIT Colony, Mylapore,
Chennai, Tamil Nadu - 600 004

First Published by Notion Press 2020
Copyright © Manoj Kumar Patel and Kshyudha S. Choudhury 2020
All Rights Reserved.

ISBN 978-1-64899-641-2

Dedicated to our respected teacher
Dr. Tej Narayan Tiwari
Professor of Physics (retired),
National Institute of Technology, Rourkela, India

Contents

Acknowledgement

Blessings and teachings of noble souls improvise and reinforce succeeding generations. The good intents and good deeds of pure hearts and developed minds have kept this universe sailing smooth even in difficult phases when the entire humanity has faced challenges from within and outside. Leaders, scientists and researchers are doing innovative work on a war footing, while the entire humanity is battling to survive the apparently unconquerable attack of the invisible Covid-19 virus.

Detractors and negative minds, on the other hand, are obstacles to good doers. But doers and intelligent humans accept the critics in positive spirit. Detractors often work as catalysts to put the projects of innovators on the fast track, with more determination.

We thankfully acknowledge their points of view because a step forward necessarily needs pressure from behind, and this is provided by detractors.

We thankfully acknowledge the great souls, the frontline warriors – nurses, doctors, paramedical staff, essential services providers, and police personal – in taming Covid-19 and saving humans lives. We also thank the women – the most precious and admirable creation of the Almighty – who, in the form of sisters, mothers and daughters – gave us the determination and courage to write this book.

We thankfully acknowledge the typesetting and photographs selections of Gayatri who gave us motherly advices in her peculiar youthful but shy mannerisms.

We thank the buyers and readers of this book. We are thankful to you for choosing it from a list of books and giving it a read.

We also acknowledge the team at Notion Press, Mr. Suriya Narayanan and Ms. Jeevlin in particular, for their all-out efforts in publishing the book on the auspicious day of the Ratha Jatra of the Almighty Mahaprabhu Shree Jagannatha on the 23rd day in the month of June 2020.

Manoj Kumar Patel
Kshyudha S Choudhury

Preface

Literature shows an infinite number of game-changing concepts that are extremely useful for peace, progress, stability and development of human race along with the sustainability and wellbeing of other living beings and Mother Nature. A close look at the success stories in the areas of economics, science, technology, medicine, mining and society reveals that 'thinking' can change history and the way we live.

In the battlefield of Kurukshetra, Arjuna, the expectant and eager warrior, looking to kill Duryodhana and Karna, resorted to distort thinking. Suddenly, right in the battlefield, he refused to fight against the Kauravas. He forgot his duties and the very purpose of the war. Sri Krishna then reminded him of his role in the war. It was not a fight between the Pandavas and the Kauravas for wealth and kingdom. Sri Krishna explained to Arjuna that the purpose of the war was to establish righteousness over evil. The war was being fought to eliminate the evil-doers and start a new and healthy society on the face of the earth. The war was to bring the dawn of a peaceful era after a long time. Sri Krishna emphasized with brilliant logic that the war was not to be contemplated by Arjuna as a fight between brothers. Each warrior on either side was supreme. But unless the war was fought and the evils were eliminated, the establishment of righteousness was impossible, Sri Krishna reiterated. Otherwise, the world and several innocent people, then and in the future, would suffer because of evil powers. Arjuna was then convinced. He raised his bow, *the Gandiva*, and the arrows, and got ready for the war.

The discussion between Arjuna and Sri Krishna, just before the beginning of the Mahabharata War, has been compiled in the form of a course called **Gita**. The explanation of Sri Krishna, with an aim to clarify the doubts and questions raised by Arjuna, is an example of **Design Thinking**. (Note that the questions of Arjuna were subtly different from one another.) It is this thinking that changed the course of mankind forever. So, the subject of design thinking is as old as the Mahabharata, which is about 6,500 years old.

Great kings, philosophers, scientist and leaders across the world, over the course of the past thousands of years, have changed the normal paths of progress and development through new ideas and newer ways of doing things. All these are resplendent examples of design thinking.

It is a different matter that the term 'design thinking' was not in use back then. These two words have perhaps been in use only since the 1960s. But the subject of design thinking has been present in concept and practice for a long time, i.e. from thousands of years ago.

Understanding the intent of great minds is difficult. That is the reason many culturally rich civilizations got destroyed. The Vedic culture, the Mohenjo-daro and Harappa civilization, the *Sanatana* culture, the Roman culture, and many more civilizations that reached the pinnacle of growth and a technologically advanced stage have crumbled with the passage of time. The culture depicted in the form of great literature like the Vedas was too esoteric to be understood by the common citizenry. There was lack of print and writing media during those days. So people tried to remember the great epics through memory. Over a period of time, there were only a handful of people who could really understand the difficult language of the Vedas. These handful people perhaps twisted many facts to their convenience. They employed twisted interpretations to earn an income. That is the time period when the Mahabharata, of which the Gita is a part, was written down by Veda Vyas. The written form is a gist of the Vedas. This is another example of design thinking that imparts unbiased knowledge to generations in an untwisted form.

In the past, Galileo and many other scientists had to keep their scientific work away from society, which was controlled by religious organizations. The scientific and technological inventions that we read about in our general science classes are the results of design thinking during the course of generations. But for Bohr and Rutherford, there could not have been the modern form of the atomic theory. But for the attempts of the Wright brothers, there could not have been spaceships. But for Archimedes, there could not have been advanced methods of applications of density measurement and purity determination of metals. But for resource availability, there could not have been a Mission Mars by ISRO.

The topic of design thinking is a time-tested and age-old concept. The only issue is it has been applied in bits and pieces on subject-specific ways. It is, thus, necessary to compile the entire concept into a capsular form and study this subject as a thought-provoking material. This could be the basis of development in all branches of science, commerce, medicine, technology and society. Today, as we struggle to come out of the curse of the pandemic caused by the Covid-19 virus, it is only design thinking that can help in developing a vaccine for this virus.

Knowledge of the subject of design thinking is not an option but a necessity. Routine thinking cannot sustain the need and greed of population and population explosion. Each one has to think differently to make a change in the way life is lived.

This book emphasizes the need for design thinking and the application of design thinking in the areas of agriculture, mining, industry and entrepreneurship. We shall be covering more areas in subsequent editions of the book.

We hope that our attempt to delve into the area of design thinking will prove useful to readers.

Manoj Kumar Patel
Rourkela

Introduction

Human beings are blessed – for the first two decades of their lives can be used completely to adapt, study and learn. The home is the first place where a child learns to adapt with others. Pre-school and kindergarten are the stages when the child learns to socialize. Then follows life in schools and colleges, where one studies different subjects. After college education, people are left to themselves to find sustenance and development. The post-college period is when each individual, consciously or subconsciously, steps up to reach the level of self-actualization. Education is the passport to enter the professional sphere. This passport is useful to obtain a visa to a particular profession only when the person concerned is ready with something different. This 'something different' is the set of characteristics and skills that gives a person an edge over the others to get picked during the selection (interview or screening) process. Not strangely enough, this set of 'something different' is not taught in the curriculum of schools and colleges.

The environment at homes, schools, colleges, playgrounds, social arenas, and other areas offers huge opportunities to learn from the skills, idiosyncrasies, dumbness, alacrity, gregariousness, solitariness, selfishness and altruism of others. These factors provide unhindered and limitless scope for learning through observations. One who can understand and learn from these is the one who makes himself 'different'. Now, strangely enough, the education and training systems in vogue eat away the unconventional learning processes in students, whose brains are most adaptable and receptive.

Scoring good grades in formal education is not an indicator of innovative and out-of-the-box thinking. Students from educational institutes that encourage practical and socially acceptable projects as part of the grading system do exceptionally well in their life compared to students who get an A+ grade solely on academic performances. Sometimes, even the A+ grade holders find themselves in difficult situations because:

a.   They grew up with systems that emphasized on theoretical and bookish knowledge.
b.   They followed and recognized sheer classroom examination formats as a means of recognition and
c.   They were not exposed to the practical world that demands practice rather than theories.

Professionals broadly termed 'earth movers', deal with mining, excavation, tunnel building, large-scale water transfers, and construction of roads and bridges in difficult terrains. These earth movers are from the areas of high-energy materials, mining, tunnelling and large-scale water transfers. Miners are engaged in the removal of the top surface of the earth to expose and take out precious materials like coal, copper, iron ore, granite stone, marbles stones, and gold metal. They also dig oil wells for oil and gases. Another group of professionals deal with the amendment of the strata beneath the earth. They create tunnels in the mountain ranges and tunnels below the sea level. Another set of people do the tough and challenging task of changing the course of water streams in rivers for the main purpose of large-scale water transfers, so that water-scarce areas can get water from water-surplus areas. Another task is hydropower generation by making the water streams in hilly areas to fall from the top of the hills, step down levels, and generate electricity through turbines. Mining is the subject that prepares individuals to deal with such tasks. Theories, mathematical calculations, and case studies are taught to students pursuing mining engineering degrees in colleges.

Another faculty namely 'geology and applied geology' is devoted to the knowledge of the earth's surface and below. Changing and amending positions of geological and natural entities like hills, rivers, off shores, and areas below the sea bed are tough tasks. These activities entail tremendous amount of work to be done on natural entities, and are possible only through mechanical means. But use of machines to apply mechanical forces on nature is highly difficult and, in most cases, even impossible. Thus, a faculty of science dealing with energy materials comes into the picture. Energy materials are studied, manufactured and used by a group commonly known as 'professionals in thermodynamics'. These professionals use chemicals, which convert the chemical energy stored inside them into mechanical energy to do mechanical work.

Nature is unpredictable and working on it is akin to initiating and completing projects on a continuous basis under uncertainties. Theoretical and classroom lectures are insufficient in these fields. One has to think differently to deal with and progress on the projects. Design thinking is imperative and is not an option for professionals involved in earth moving. We shall discuss some real-life cases related to this field in the subsequent sections.

01

Design Thinking

Design thinking has been associated with us since time immemorial. It can be dated back to the earliest era of human existence when man applied the senses of sight, smell and touch to select food from trees for survival. The process got sharpened during subsequent periods as the sense organs started knowing better the tastes of ripe fruits and burnt meat. So, design thinking is an old process.

If design thinking is an old subject and it is already available within us, then the question that arises is: why study it now as a part of the syllabus in schools and colleges, as prescribed now by the Central Board of Secondary Education (CBSE)?

The entire universe that our eyes can see and the mind can perceive and that our eyes cannot see and the mind cannot perceive is filled with an infinite number of complex matters—both live and non-living. The general tendency of living beings is to explore better ways to find safety, comfort, simplicity and happiness. This inherent tendency has given rise to habitats of different types—such as cool dark places for reptiles, forests for animals, and cleaner and easily accessible places for humans. Further, the ever curious human brain has evolved from the Stone Age to the present digital age. Humans are always in search of enjoyment without efforts. Thus, they discovered places, edibles and agriculture for their basic needs. Thereafter, and maybe side by side, they invented machines—from boats to travel from one place to another to space vehicles to travel from earth to extra-terrestrial locations. Humans also invented means of entertainment—starting with radio, then television, and beyond. The human brain started inventing means to communicate within groups and outside groups. Thus came about inventions such as the telegram and now the all-pervading mobile phone. Man's ultimate aim to become happy has somehow taken his mindset to become the master of the universe. So, the human brain is continuously thinking of doing things better and in a superior way. Thus, the process of development lies in thinking. It is well understood that if you can think, then you can do. This is the basic point for which we have to design the thinking process.

The complexity of interrelations between parameters in nature and other entities have incited man to discover, invent and develop new matter, products, processes and services. So, hitherto simple things started becoming compartmentalised into basic things. For example, today there are specialized branches of medical sciences dealing separately with the retina, laceration and pupil, which were earlier limited to one branch called ENT. Today, ENT is a combination of areas such as otology, rhinology, laryngology, rhinoplasty and pinnaplasty. In order to develop and invent, professionals in their respective fields are required to think continuously. But our education system at the basic levels such school and high school is mostly core subject oriented. There is emphasis on physics, chemistry, mathematics, economics, computer science, natural environment, political science, so on and so forth. Unfortunately, very little emphasis is given to topics such as physical activities, yoga, prayer and thinking differently. Intelligent quotient or IQ is given importance over emotional quotient or EG. Interpersonal relationships are an important factor after the college period; but it is not taught as a part of the curriculum. Entrepreneurship as a possible industry like agriculture and manufacturing has never been inculcated in the minds of young school – and college-going students. "Thinking" as a prerequisite to development has not been emphasized upon. The negative outcomes of ignoring these basic characteristics in the education system are:

a. developing the brain as a repository of mere theoretical knowledge, and

b. distancing individuals from one another.

But training the brain to think is of importance and hence design thinking is now appropriately thought of as a core subject in the curriculum of high schools. Surely, it will flow down to the levels of school curricula. Design thinking as a core subject will enable educational institutes to deliver better individuals to society.

Earlier, industrial jobs earlier were labour-intensive basically for two reasons. The first reason is the easy availability of abundant human labour and the second reason is the unavailability of automation. As time passed, mechanization and automation came into practice, which was quickly succeeded by digital operations. At the same time, availability of skilled manpower to operate machines became difficult. The process of automation has moved faster than the pace at which man can adapt and adopt to it. Thus, process owners in industries became dependent on manpower. This dependency gave rise to higher costs of production because skilled operators demanded high salaries and wages. Unconsciously, rather than consciously, process owners tried hard to reduce their dependency on manpower. They looked for machines that could be operated by anyone trained for a very short period of time.

Thus, replacing manpower with machines resulted in two big advantages. In the first place, costs arising out of manpower deployment were drastically reduced. Secondly, machines started yielding higher production with better consistency. Process variations were controlled. Now all process owners in fields such as manufacturing, services, research and development, agriculture, and space research have realized that more and more replacement of manpower with machines is a better way to get results with higher production, higher productivity, more precision, lesser wastages, and, above all, best and consistent quality i.e. six sigma and beyond. At the same time, better products and processes can come into existence only when people start thinking and conceptualizing based on their thinking. Thus, thinking as a subject in the curricula of schools and high schools will mould fertile and fresh brains to make inventions and developments faster. Thus, there is a strong reason to study design thinking.

Gone are the days when wars were fought to acquire and amass wealth. Now strategic plans are made and executed to create wealth. Economists can design a plan that can ease the flow of money from other nations to their nations. Think of life insurance companies. People working in these companies devise and offer plans to people where both the insurer and the insuree are benefitted financially. This is an example of design thinking that involves thinking differently. Today, pharmaceutical companies are investing heavily in research and development activities so as to prepare medicines and antibiotics that are superior with fewer side effects, a quicker response time, and a lesser cost. These companies do not have to steal the ideas of others or peep into the laboratories of other companies. They are hiring people who can think differently and formulate medicines and antibiotics of superior quality at a lesser cost. The year 2019 ended with the beginning of a disaster, creating a virus called Novel Corona or Covid-19.

Originating from the Wuhan city of China, the virus has caused a pandemic in all the countries across the world. It has taken the lives of millions. The entire world is caught unprepared. Scientists in research laboratories across the nations are struggling to find a medicine for this virus but they are yet to find anything. So, it is now 'thinking' that would help scientists develop a suitable medicine. This development would be possible only through thinking. If we do not prepare our young brains to think differently, then it will be difficult for them to develop and invent products and processes in the future. Today, all medicines are set aside and the only one that is most sought-after is a medicine to kill the Covid-19 virus.

We shall discuss the application of design thinking in a large number of areas in this book. Our deliberations will run through the subject areas of:

1. Social innovation
2. Education system
3. Personal and personality development
4. Research and development
5. Drug discovery and new molecule inventions
6. Agriculture
7. Manufacturing industries
8. Service, hospitality and tourism industries
9. Mining industries
10. Health and nutraceutical sectors
11. Other prospective and newer areas such as defence, marketing, economics, public distribution system, and religion as education

This book is expected to be useful in reinforcing the foundation of the education system and building future citizens of capabilities. Thus, the attempt is invest in the head rather in the hand.

Design thinking

Design thinking (DT) is inherent, and our own beliefs are that every living being inherently possesses this characteristic. However, like other areas of learning, this too needs to be realized, trained, and used as a part of the learning process. Animals and all living beings use this characteristic to keep themselves alive, and this can be best appreciated when we realize that they survive even when their places of survival are encroached by humans for comforts – desired and undesired. Since living beings, other than humans, use the inherent characteristics raw, untrained and unsharpened, they disappear from the face of the earth. We humans have named this *pattern of disappearance* as 'survival of the fittest'. But the 'fittest' comes from the very process of design thinking. Humans design their *thinking* to clear up spaces of wild and other animals and make them their own spaces to survive. This is the first and basic example of design thinking.

Human nature with respect to power, sex and wealth is insatiable. The more humans get something, the more they yearn for it. Thus begins the race for more and more. Getting more than what one has and the greed to acquire more than what is needed are possible only when plans and strategies are made. Plans and strategies arise from thinking, more specifically DT.

So, DT is to garner more from existing resources. It is to get 'unlimited' from the use of 'limited'. DT is a concept that is age-old. Today DT has become an application in all branches of studies such as anthropology, sociology, economics, and science and technology by involving computer science and information technology. But it was present in the form of common sense, mathematics and statistics for a very long time.

We can also call it Plan-Do-Check-Act (PDCA). It starts with identification of a problem and then necessarily following the steps of conceptualization, analysis, model making, and then acting. We shall see this from the points of IT as well as non-IT views.

Origin and timeline of design thinking

The topic of design thinking is very old. It is necessary to study this subject as a thought-provoking material. This could be the basis of development in all branches of science, commerce, medicine, technology and society. Today, as we are struggling to come out of the curse of the pandemic caused by the Covid-19 virus, it is only design thinking that can help in developing an antibody for this virus.

Design thinking's origin dates back to thousands of years ago. Its origin has been traced back to the post-Vedic period. However, the scientific community needs a proof from established record-keeping sources. Thus, it is our scientific responsibility to draw the timeline with respect to the records available in the history of science and technology.

Great kings, philosophers, scientist and leaders all over the world, during the course of the last thousands of years, have changed the normal path of progress and development through design thinking. It is a different matter that the term 'design thinking' was not in use back then. These two words have been in use perhaps since the 1960s.

In 1969, American sociologist and psychologist Herbert Simon published an article that is said to have laid the foundations for design thinking. In *The Sciences of the Artificial*, Simon set out seven key steps for using design as a creative approach to problem solving. This seven-stage model is highly reminiscent of the five-stage process commonly used today.

Another key figure in shaping the design thinking process is design theorist Horst Rittel. In the 1970s, Rittel coined the term 'wicked problems' to describe complex problems that are tricky to define, have no set number of potential solutions, and tend to be symptomatic of another problem.

Design theorist Richard Buchanan connected Rittel's wicked problems to design thinking in the early 90s when he published the book *Wicked Problems in Design Thinking*.

In the early 90s, international design and consulting firm IDEO was founded. IDEO is often hailed as one of the most instrumental drivers in bringing design thinking to the mainstream. The IDEO Design Thinking model divides the process into three key phases: inspiration, ideation and implementation.

In the early 2000s, design thinking was introduced as a course at the university level. A notable leader in this field was the Stanford School of Design (or the Standford d.school), which began teaching design thinking in 2005.

Train thinking

The age-old wisdom is 'think before you act'. The most difficult thing is 'thinking' or 'to think'.

If you can think, then you can solve. If you think, you can address any issue holistically. The problem solving process is as unlimited as one can think of in daily life. If you think that you have to wake up at 3 a.m. in the morning, then you will get up at 3 a.m. by setting your biological clock accordingly. In the same token, the part of the human that does the thinking and processing is the best part, i.e. the brain. The brain, unfortunately, unlike the heart, prefers to be at rest. The brain is lazy. The heart does not need training to function and pump blood. But the brain needs a lot of training to think. Every human has got more or less the same size of brain and the same number of neurons. But only a selected few become developed like Aryabhatta, Charaka, Arjuna, Einstein, Stephen Hawking, Emerson, Newton, Shakespeare and Kalidasa. It is because they trained and aligned their brain to think differently. They asked "why not" rather than "why". So, we need to train the mind to think.

A learner-centric atmosphere encourages participants (students, peers, employees) to get loosened from the narrow, rigid and water-tight processes of learning. It incentivizes the individuals who think out of the box to capitalize on the learner-centred principles of connection-making, inquiry and self-directed learning. In such an environment, integration gets built up as participants construct knowledge through inquiry, doing to learn, making mistakes, and becoming more self-directed. So, the atmosphere transits from content delivery (the gradation system we may refer) and nice end products to building participants' capacity by co-creating learning goals and realizing to make the learning process the primary focus.

In spite of Despite temptation, paucity of space and the desire to focus on the hard-core subject refrain the author from discussing the teaching system and training processes followed during ancient times, may be with respect to civilizations during the period of the Ramayana, Mahabharata, Romans, Indus Valley, Vana Vidyalaya (open school in Odisha), and Shantiniketan, which were forerunners in design thinking. We shall not discuss this area in further detail, but we can conclude that thinking process can be guided and trained in order to practise in an unconsciously conscious manner.

The first choice of the searching process—Google—throws up about 73,90,00,000 results related to the topic 'training in design thinking' in just 0.65 seconds. The sheer numbers from the search engine are a proof that there are more than enough data in the repository of libraries that speak and deliberate on 'training and design thinking'. It is thus unnecessary for us to deal with definitions and subject contents in the general sense.

However, here are ten of the best training programmes on the subject.

1. Mastering Design Thinking (MIT Management Executive Education)
2. Design Thinking Certification for Innovation (Coursera)
3. Managing Innovation and Design Thinking by HEC Paris (Coursera)
4. Design Thinking Certification Program by Rochester Institute (edX)
5. MIT's Approach to Design Thinking (MIT Management Executive Education)
6. Diploma in Innovation & Design Thinking (Columbia Business School)
7. Design Thinking Certification for Business Strategy & Entrepreneurship (Coursera)
8. Cooper Crash Course: Designing Thinking in 3 Steps (Udemy)
9. Agile Meets Design Thinking by University of Virginia (Coursera)
10. Learning Design Thinking (LinkedIn Learning)

The above list is only a miniscule part of the entire spectrum on the subject. We will now discuss some of the steps that can facilitate DT.

Advantages of design thinking

The design thinking process puts the needs and requirements of the user first. In a nutshell, the design thinking process enables you to find innovative solutions to complex problems, driven by the needs of the target user.

Some of the benefits of the design thinking process are:

- **The design thinking process teaches people how to innovate and solve problems.**

While most of us are programmed to solve problems that readily present themselves, we're not necessarily inclined to go looking for problems. Design thinking encourages creative problem solving; it pushes you to redefine the problem space and seek out the challenge that is really worth solving. This is especially useful in a business context—whether it's designing a competitive digital product, optimizing internal processes, or reinventing an entire business model.

- **The design thinking process fosters teamwork and collaboration.**
Innovations and answers to complex questions are best generated in a heterogeneous team of people. The design thinking process brings multidisciplinary teams together, breaks down the problem, and encourages people to collaborate and reach a solution through debate and experiments with regard to challenging their assumptions.

- **The design thinking process offers a proven competitive advantage.**
The aim of the design thinking process is to come up with solutions, products, or services that are desirable for the user, economically viable from a business perspective, and technologically feasible. This user-first approach coupled with early and frequent testing helps to minimize risks, drive customer engagement, and ultimately boost the bottom line.

Design thinking is a tool for creativity, innovation, and problem solving. Not only does it help designers to come up with ground-breaking products, it also fosters a culture of innovation and user-centricity at every level of the business.

Steps in design thinking

Thus, design thinking is an analytical and creative process that engages a person in opportunities to experiment, create prototype models, gather feedback, and redesign. The learner possesses rights, is an active constructor of knowledge, and is a social being. The instructor is a collaborator and co-learner along with the child, a guide and facilitator, and a researcher.

The five steps involved in design thinking are: Empathize, Define, Ideate, Prototype and Test. Design thinking is aimed at solving the problems from the user's point of view. In the simplest of the form, let us suppose a region is fast losing water from agricultural land through potential evapotranspiration (PET). Then the need of the people is to find a solution to this problem. Agro scientists and meteorologists would attempt to solve this problem. These would be the steps they would follow to solve this problem.

They would attempt to understand the problem by empathizing with the pain points of people. → They need to convert the ground level problem into a technical form (remember the House of Quality or Quality Function

Deployment). → They would brainstorm and generate ideas to solve the problem. → They would carry out experiments in laboratories through samples and prototypes. → Finally, they would carry out field trials to find the efficacy of the ideated method (remember the Plan-Do-Check-Act PDCA cycle).

Stage 1: Empathize i.e. understand the need of the user

The first stage of the design thinking process necessitates the problem solver to gain an empathetic understanding of the problem that he is trying to solve. This step could be simple or complex depending upon the type of the problem. If the researcher is trying to solve air pollution during the festival of lights, then he will have to empathetically understand the pains of people.

Empathy is crucial to a human-centric design process like design thinking because it allows the de-bottlenecker to set aside his own assumptions and biases.

If the The words from the statement "I can understand the grief you are experiencing" are reflected in the eyes of the aggrieved then it is an example of empathy. Author Bhaavna Arora in her book titled *Undaunted: Lt Ummer Fayaz of Kashmir* has mentioned that tears welled up in her eyes and her voice choked when she met with the family members of Lt Ummer Fayaz for the first time. She wanted to speak to the family so that she could put feelings into the words while writing her proposed book on the lieutenant. The aggrieved sister Asmat could feel the empathy from Bhaavna. Then conversation between them was effective.

We shall take one of the very recent incidents as another example to understand 'empathy'. From the beginning of the year 2020 and till date i.e. June 2020, India, like most of the other countries in the world, has been passing through a very difficult time. The number of infections and painful deaths due to the novel Corona virus Covid-19 are on the rise. As a containment measure, the Government of India decided to lockdown activities in order to facilitate physical distancing at the workplace. Despite all its good intents and expected good results, the lockdown, which began with effect from the last week of March 2020, made millions of workmen jobless. Jobless individuals and their family members suffered due to lack of shelter and food. To add to that, the hot summer began as usual, from mid-March and continued till the middle of June. Heat from up above i.e. the sun, and the fire of hunger from the empty stomach made these poor people take certain decisions to save their lives and the lives of their family members. They desperately looked for ways and means to move out and reach their homelands with a hope of at least getting food to survive. The migration of millions of workmen with their families thus started and the need was to survive somehow. These acts were empathized by many people sitting in the decision taking positions.

Empathy is thus the first step in the subject of design thinking.

Stage 2: Define i.e. convert the problem to a technical form

In the subject of Total Quality Management (TQM), there are two areas namely, The House of Quality and Quality Function Deployment (QFD). This approach necessitates the definition of the layman description of a problem into a technical format. For example, if the users mention that the toothpaste is becoming flowy after storing the tube for about seven days, then the problem solver (design thinker) has to accept take this input and convert it into technical language. In this particular case, the technical definition is: toothpaste pertaining to batch numbers 'xxxxx' to 'uuuuu' has got de-emulsified. This problem is now well-defined and technical experts will solve it by following the succeeding three stages.

In the 'define' stage, the de-bottlenecker draws and accumulates the information available during the 'empathize' stage. He analyzes the observations and synthesizes them to define the core problem.

Continuing from the two examples discussed in the previous paragraphs, the problem definition can be understood.

In the first example, the conversation between the visitor and Asmat came to the stage of *definition* after *empathy*. The relevant points are defined here.

Similarly, in the second example pertaining to the migration of workmen and their family members, empathy could be defined properly only after their hardships and miseries were felt with empathy by the policy-makers and decision-makers. Thus, the problems were defined as the results of the following:

a.   They were thrown out by their employers.
b.   They suddenly stopped earning.
c.   They were thrown into uncertainties.
d.   They wanted to be with their dear ones during the pandemic.

Stage 3: Ideate i.e. create ideas

This stage is also known as ideation. Here the designers generate ideas through brainstorming, experiences, rules of thumb, and discussions with experts. The solid background of knowledge from the first two phases facilitates and strengthens idea generation by thinking 'outside the box'.

The reason for the flowy toothpaste, as discussed in one of the previous paragraphs, is de-emulsification. Having understood the reasons, the design thinker would solve the problem by adopting the rights steps and procedures. In this particular instance of flowing gel, the ideation process will proceed as follows.

The design thinkers will find the details of the problematic batches. They will trace the said batches and find out that they were manufactured in process plant 'vvvv'. The ideation will generate points with respect to the following:

a.   quality of the emulsifier used during manufacture of the batch of toothpaste
b.   process conditions maintained during manufacture
c.   quality of input materials
d.   SOPs
e.   operator deployed during manufacture

Thus, the design thinker defines, through ideation, the possible reason for the flowy toothpaste: poor quality of emulsifier used during the manufacturing of the said batch. So, the products may be called back from the market. In future, quality with respect to the emulsifier has to be tightened.

Coming to the example of the book, *Undaunted: Lt Ummer Fayaz of Kashmir*, the idea of penning down the right words was generated here by the visitor or the writer of the book.

In the second example regarding the migrant workers too, the ideation step was followed. The decision-makers and the policy-makers generated ideas to: (a) solve the problem and (b) address the ramifications of the problems arising out of the migration of workers. The ideas were to:

a.   contain the workers and their families in their respective places to the extent possible by convincing them and assuring them of supply of food, shelter and clothing,

b.   devise means to run trains and transport systems in a controlled manner, and

c.   place them in their hometowns and villages with quarantine so as to stop accidental spread of the virus in the areas.

The next step was to implement the ideas in a controlled manner and see the efficacy.

Stage 4: Prototype i.e. results of experimentation

This is an experimental phase. Here the aim is to identify the best possible solution for each of the problems identified during the first three stages. The case discussed here narrowed down the reason for de-emulsification to the poor quality of the emulsifier. A number of experiments will be carried out to establish the validity of the assumption. Each experiment will give rise to a 'sample' or 'prototype'.

Observation of the exodus of migrant workers with their families and steps taken by administration and governments provides a good understanding of the prototype or pre-final stage. Initially, students stuck in places like Kota were brought back by deploying dedicated bus services. This step was found to be effective and successful to a large extent. The process was then scaled up for large transfers of migrant workmen and their families.

Prototyping thus facilitates the design thinkers to finetune the product, process and services before launching the final products and finalizing the processes and services.

Stage 5: Test i.e. coming out with the solution

Designers or evaluators will rigorously test the complete product using the best solutions identified in the prototype phase. This is the final phase of the model. In this particular case, finally the product, i.e. good emulsified toothpaste, is released in the market. But, in an iterative process such as design thinking, the results generated are often used to *redefine* one or more problems. Designers can then choose to return to the previous stages of the process to make further iterations, alterations and refinements to rule out alternative solutions, which are identical to the Plan-Do-Check-Act or the PDCA cycle.

That is how we as consumers get good products and services from manufacturers and service providers. The simplest example of product innovation through design thinking are the smartphones that are launched with myriad new features every six-twelve months. Online services, such as purchase and home delivery of products and services through software applications, in the form of Uber, Ola and Amazon are results of design thinking. The correction suggestions and the spell checks in Microsoft Word is another example of design thinking.

We discussed two examples in this section. We may conclude that the final shape that these examples took were planned by the design thinkers—the writer of the book in the first case and the people behind the implementation of solutions for the transport of workmen and their families in the second case.

In the first case, the writer could write a very nicely articulated great book namely *Undaunted: Lt Ummer Fayaz of Kashmir*. The rating of this book in Amazon Kindle is 4.7 in a scale of 5, as on 29th of May 2020.

In the second example, that is the one related to the transport of migrant workmen, the governments at the Centre and in the states implemented the final steps by ways of:

a.   running Shramik Special Trains for the ease of movement of people to their home states,

b.   provision of supply of foods and water bottles in the stations, and

c.   opening up of sheltering places in schools and community centres (some of the short-term measures).

Having understood the terms and subject of design thinking, we shall now proceed to see its applications in different branches of science and technology. As we proceed to individual chapters, the reader will find each chapter split into different sections. The sections are well connected to give a background of the core subject followed by applications in the said core subject. We shall deliberate on the areas of mining, agriculture and entrepreneurship. These three areas have been selected because they are spoken of less though they are important and have highly demanding innovations. Any country, like and unlike India, that has a high scope of economic development through sustainable exploration of natural resources and agriculture has to emphasize entrepreneurship in these areas.

02

Design Thinking in Environment Management

Introduction

The environment in its widest sense is called the biosphere. This consists of the earth's crust, the surrounding atmosphere, and the various forms of life that exist in the zone between 600 m above and 10,000 m below the sea level. The biosphere is very large and complex, and so it is usually divided into smaller units or ecosystems. The concept of ecosystem is defined as the plants, animals and micro-organisms that live in a defined zone, and the physical factors present in it, such as soil, water and air. Within an ecosystem, such as a river, there exist dynamic interrelationships between the living forms and their physical environment.

These relationships can be expressed as natural cycles that provide a continuous circulation of the essential constituents necessary for life. The cycles mainly operate in a balanced state, with little variation in the unpolluted natural environment. If this natural balance did not exist, then many life-sustaining processes would not be maintained and the ecosystem would be variable and unstable. The balanced operation of the natural cycles and ecosystems contributes to the stability of the entire biosphere, which is fundamental to the continued existence and development of life on earth.

These natural cycles are:

a. Hydrological cycle
b. Nitrogen cycle
c. Phosphate cycle
d. Sulphur cycle
e. Oxygen cycle

The hydrological cycle is a continuous natural process wherein water is exchanged between the atmosphere, the land, the sea, all living plants and animals, and industrial plants. This cycle consists of a balanced continuous process of evaporation, transpiration, precipitation, surface run-off, and ground water movements.

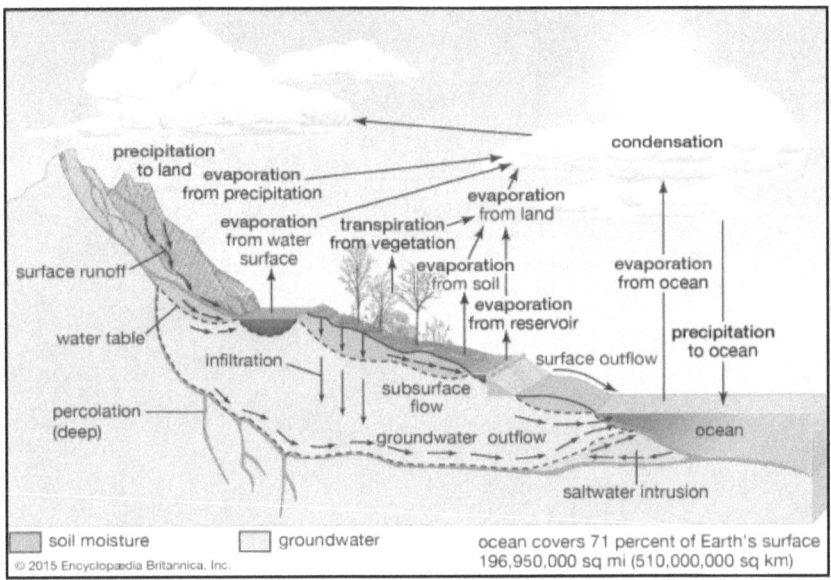

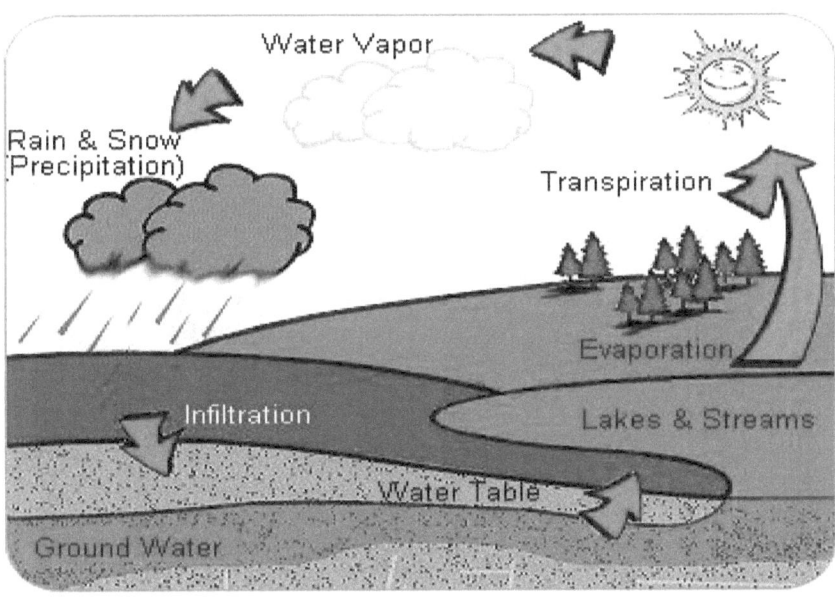

The presence of nitrogen and its compounds in the biosphere is essential for the maintenance of life. Exchange of nitrogen takes place within ecosystems constituting the nitrogen cycle. The process of nitrogen cycle keeps the concentration of nitrogen in the atmosphere relatively constant, and thus the natural cycle is balanced.

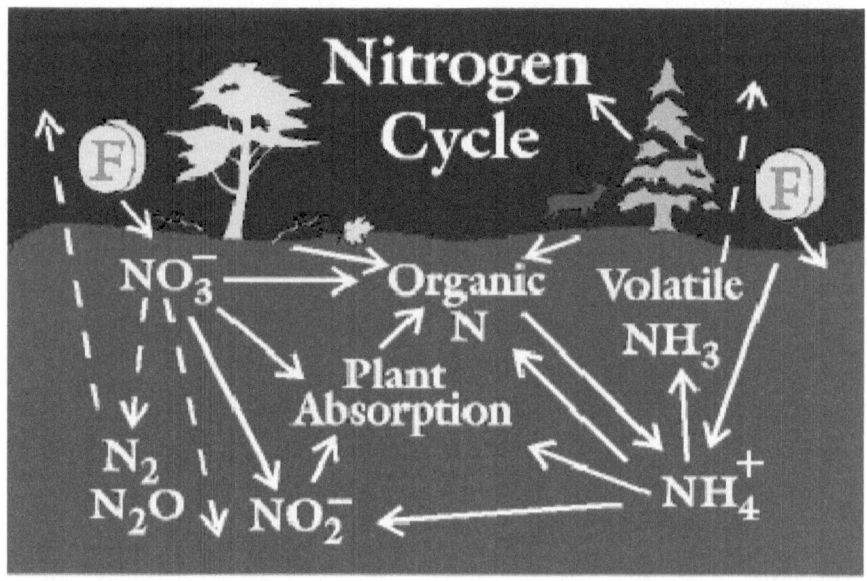

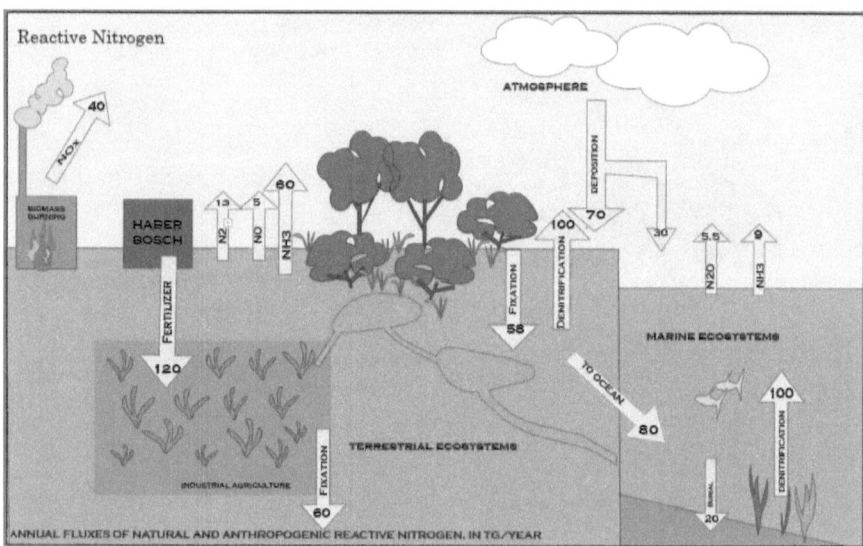

Phosphates, especially organophosphates, are essential for cell division involving the production of nuclear DNA and RNA; phosphates are also required for the growth and maintenance of animal bones and teeth. Exchange of phosphates takes place within the ecosystem through the living bodies. The circulation of phosphates and its compounds in the environment constitutes the phosphate cycle.

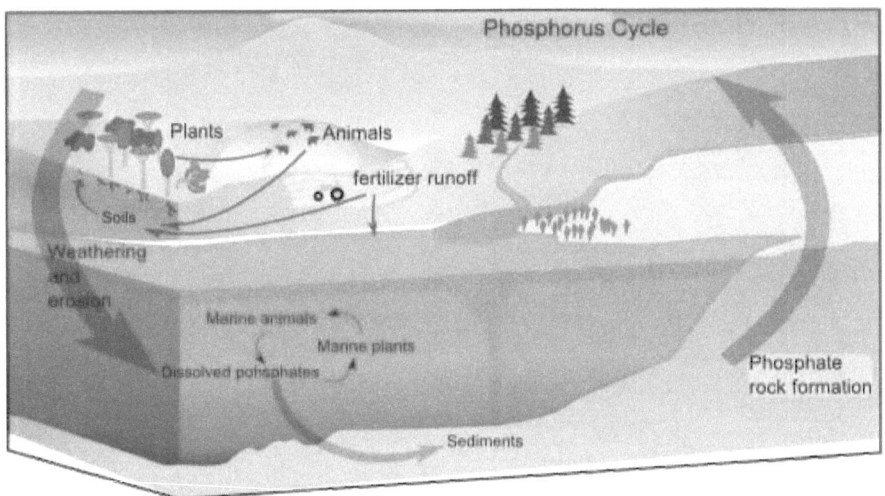

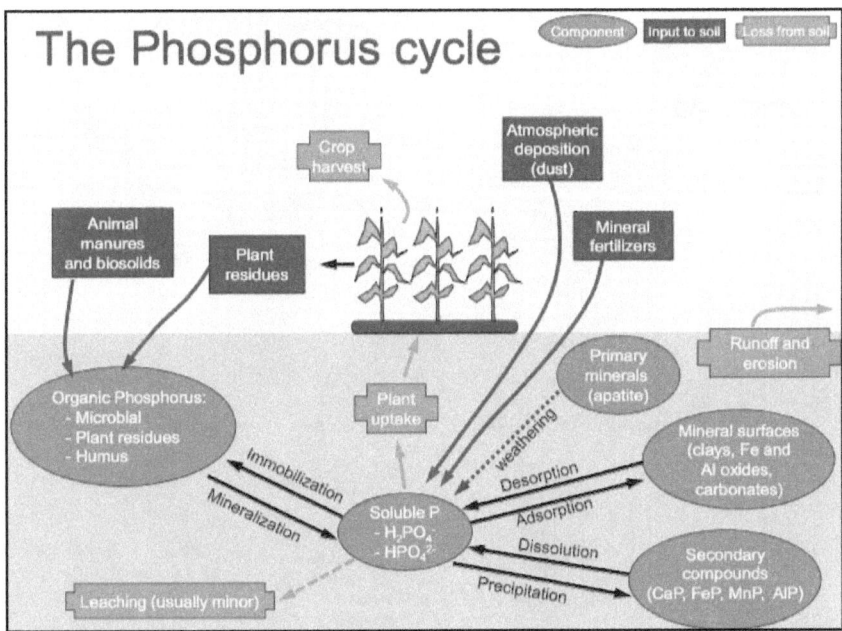

Plants and animals require a continuous supply of sulphur and its compounds in order to synthesize some amino acids and proteins. Exchanges of sulphur take place within ecosystems through the activities of the so-called sulphur bacteria. The circulation of sulphur and its compounds in the environment constitutes the sulphur cycle.

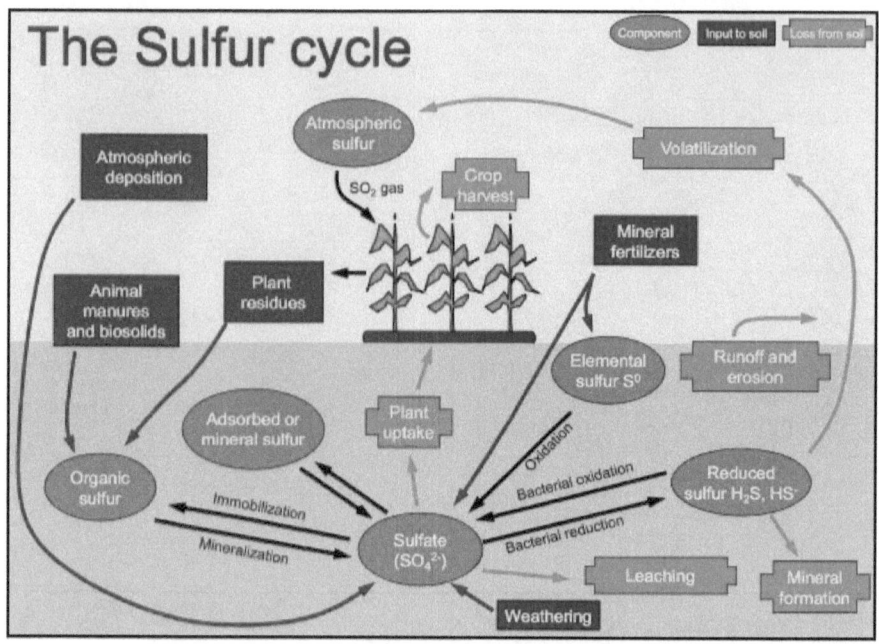

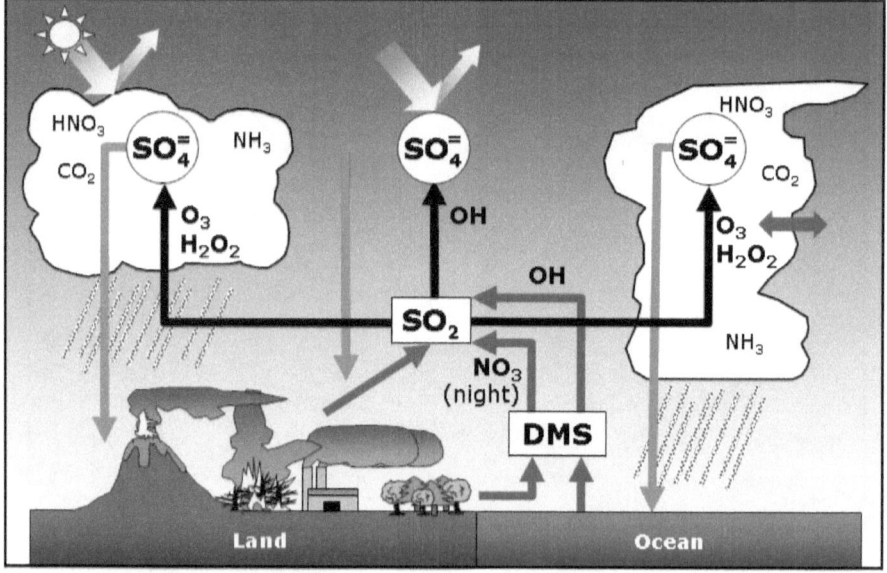

Oxygen is a major component of all living organisms and therefore an adequate supply of the gas is vital for continued life in the biosphere. Oxygen is required by most plants and animals and all humans for aerobic respiration or enzymic oxidation of organic food, which sustains growth and general metabolism. The total amount of oxygen in the biosphere is relatively constant, and the oxygen cycle is relatively stable.

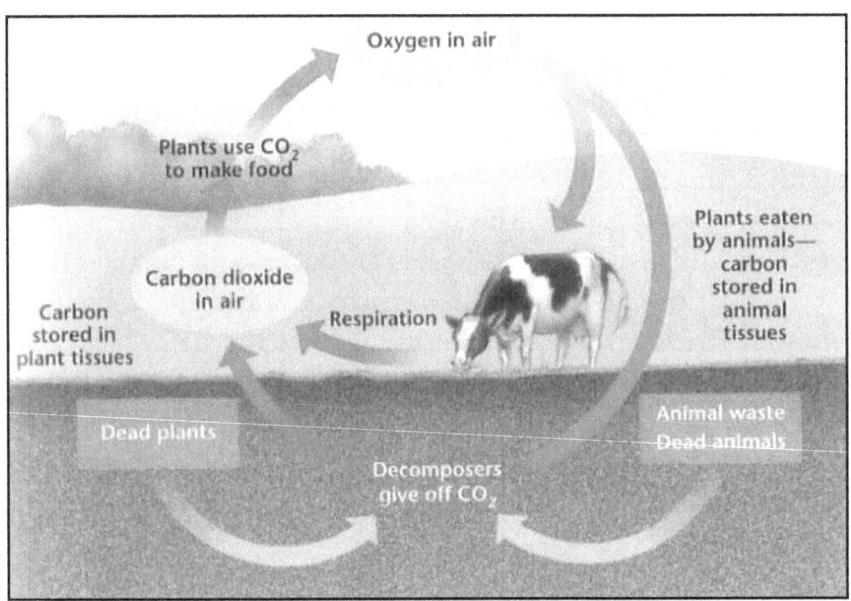

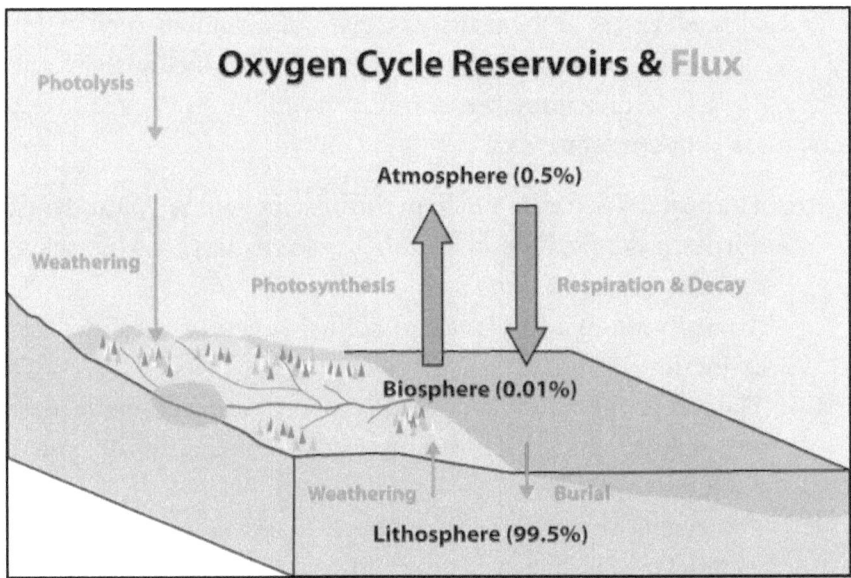

However, all the above mentioned natural cycles of the environment are prone to change from the prevailing balances due to the effect of human activities. In fact, pre-industrial production systems and various occupations and cultures, which are based on sound ecological principles, are being rapidly destroyed in the name of economic development and modernisation.

The scenario

The most distinguishing feature of the present era is that man has become the architect of his future. The unprecedented increase in population and even greater increase in the scale and intensity of human activities, which have occurred largely in this century, have been brought about by the growing mastery of science and its applications. This has produced prosperity, high standards of living, and expanded opportunities beyond what the previous generations could have imagined. But these developments have damaged and deteriorated the ecological systems and caused widespread destruction of natural resources, on which human life and wellbeing depends.

In the name of growth, fossil fuels have been burnt in abundance, chemicals harmful to the atmosphere have proliferated, poisons have been dumped on land, rivers and oceans, and natural resources such as forests have been ravaged and exploited to the extent of reducing their natural capacity for self-stabilization. As a result, mankind is confronted with several disastrous consequences.

1. The protective ozone shield in the heavily polluted latitudes of the northern hemisphere is thinning twice as fast as what scientists thought just a few years ago.
2. A minimum of 140 plant and animal species are condemned to extinction each day.
3. The atmospheric levels of heat-trapping carbon dioxide are now 26% higher than their pre-industrial concentration, and they continue to climb up.
4. The earth's surface was warmer in 2019 than in any year since record-keeping began in the mid-nineteenth century. Six of the seven warmest years on record have occurred in the 2010s.
5. Forests are vanishing at the rate of around 17 million hectares per year – an area about half the size of Finland.

6.   World population is growing by 92 million people annually – roughly equivalent to adding a Mexico each year. Of this, 88 million are being added in the developing world.

Apart from population growth, most of the other problems are caused by the need to dispose of unwanted materials (or wastes) arising from human activities. These wastes can be gaseous, solid or liquid materials that are disregarded because they have no further apparent use for the owner, industrial processor, or manufacturer. Wastes cannot be eliminated but must be disposed of and contained within the global environment. Therefore, when waste materials are released into the atmosphere, dumped on land, or discharged into streams, rivers, or the sea, they effectively cause harm to the environment.

To meet the increasing demand of time, mankind has deliberately modified the natural environment in order to improve the quality of life. Unknowingly, however, the different development activities that are undertaken, such as construction of roads, dams, airports, power plants and industrial facilities, have an adverse impact on the environment in which man lives. When studying the impact of these activities, it is tempting to recommend a moratorium of change. But certainly this is out of question, for one would not want to pay even a fraction of the price of technological stagnation. Technological change is a national necessity in the world and thus it must not be frozen. What is needed is the concept of environmental planning and management, coupled with a full understanding of environmental concepts, methods and skills.

Man, in the twentieth century, represents an intrusion on the overall balance of the processes that maintain the earth as a habitable place in the universe. This fact is recognized by man because of his concern for the environment; but along with this, the profligacy in the consumption of resources is also continuing. Thus, it is incumbent upon mankind to examine his actions and attune them so that they ensure long-term viability of the earth as a habitable planet. The study of the parameters of natural resources is a logical first step in this process, because they represent an opportunity for man to consider, in his decision-making, the effects of actions that are not accounted for in the normal market exchange of goods and services.

Nature's backlash

Industrialization and other activities like mining and construction are taking place at a very fast pace in this century than it did about 50 years ago. But, unfortunately, the past too has seen many painful instances of pollution. The theme for World Environment Day 2019 was 'air pollution'. We will try to cover the disasters of air pollution that our previous generations have suffered through.

London smog in December 1952

A period of cold weather, combined with an anticyclone and windless conditions, collected airborne pollutants—mostly arising from the use of coal—formed a thick layer of smog over the city. It lasted from Friday (December 5) to Tuesday (December 9) 1952, and then dispersed quickly when the weather changed. It killed about 12,000 people during these five days. It was certainly a form of backlash to man's disregard of nature's delicate balance.

Pea soup fog 1948

Pea soup fog (also known as a pea souper, black fog or killer fog) is a very thick and often yellowish, greenish or blackish fog caused by air pollution, containing soot particulates and the poisonous sulphur dioxide gas. This very thick smog occurs in cities and is derived from the smoke given out by the burning of soft coal for home heating and in industrial processes. Smog of this intensity is often lethal to vulnerable people such as the elderly, the very young, and those with respiratory problems. The result of this phenomenon was commonly known as 'London particular' or 'London fog'. A reversal of the idiom 'London particular' became the name for thick pea and ham soup.

History repeats itself often in many cities. On November 9, 2017, with the onset of winter, it was reported in *The Times of India*[2] that Delhi faced a health emergency as a thick layer of toxic fog hung over the city and its adjoining regions. The fog that descended on the city was similar to what London faced in December 1952, causing chaos and death. The toxic smog is called 'pea soup fog', which is a deadly mixture of vehicular pollution, dust from construction and roads, and stubble burning.

We are all aware of the menace of air pollution. So, we need to individually put in efforts over and above the efforts made by the government. As citizens, our responsibilities are high towards Mother Earth.

Donora smog 1948

The Donora smog happened in 1948 in a mill city called Donora, Pennsylvania, near Pittsburgh on River Monongahela. The smog killed about 20 people and caused respiratory problems for 6,000 people. The total population of Donora then was 14,000 people. That means about 43% people were affected with respiratory problems and 20 people died.

Donora was an industrial town with steel and zinc industries. During those fateful days (from October 27 to October 31, 1948), there was a temperature inversion.

In general, hot air travels up and cold air remains closer to the surface. But in case of temperature inversion, the pollutants get trapped in the lower area near the earth's surface. The pollutant gases like sulphuric acid, nitrogen dioxide, fluoride and dust particles and other poisonous gases remain in the area where humans (or other living beings) breathe. Thus, living beings start breathing poisonous gases, which cause severe respiratory problems and choking. It causes death too. Smog is now present in most cities. If one is not careful, a morning walk could become a suicidal walk.

Pandemic caused by the Covid-19 virus

The entire world is passing through a period not dreamt of by anyone. The statistical data on the spread of the Covid-19 virus is sickening and threatening. The number of active cases worldwide due to the virus is about 6 million and the mortality is about 0.4 million (as on May 296, 2020). The news of more and more people getting attacked by this virus every day is worrying and disturbing to each one of us. The most developed country in the world i.e. the USA is the worst affected with the highest number of mortalities. A pandemic of this nature has not been experienced by human beings of the present time. It has surpassed all previous records including the plague in 1879.

Coronavirus Cases:

3,741,489

view by country

Deaths:

258,512

Recovered:

1,247,610

Country, Other	Total Cases	New Cases	Total Deaths	New Deaths	Total Recovered	Active Cases	Serious, Critical	Tot Cases/ 1M pop	Deaths/ 1M pop	Total Tests	Tests/ 1M pop
World	3,741,489	+16,971	258,512	+485	1,247,610	2,235,367	49,242	480	33.2		
USA	1,237,761	+128	72,275	+4	200,669	964,817	16,179	3,739	218	7,727,938	23,347
Spain	250,561		25,613		154,718	70,230	2,254	5,359	548	1,932,455	41,332
Italy	213,013		29,315		85,231	98,467	1,427	3,523	485	2,246.666	37,158
UK	194,990		29,427		N/A	165,219	1,559	2,872	433	1,383.842	20,385
France	170,551		25,531		52,736	92,284	3,430	2,613	391	1,100,228	16,856
Germany	167,007		6,993		137,400	22,614	1,937	1,993	83	2,547,052	30,400
Russia	165,929	+10,559	1,537	+86	21,327	143,065	2,300	1,137	11	4,633,731	31,752
Turkey	129,491		3,520		73,285	52,686	1,338	1,535	42	1,204,421	14,281
Brazil	115,953	+1,238	7,958	+37	48,221	59,774	8,318	546	37	339,552	1,597
Iran	99,970		6,340		80,475	13,155	2,685	1,190	75	519,543	6,186
China	82,883	+2	4,633		77,911	339	26	58	3		
Canada	62,046		4,043		26,993	31,010	502	1,644	107	940,567	24,921
Peru	51,189		1,444		15,413	34,332	709	1,553	44	406,579	12,331
Belgium	50,509		8,016		12,441	30,052	646	4,358	692	456,194	39,362
India	49,436	+36	1,695	+2	14,183	33,558		36	1	1,276.781	925
Netherlands	41,087		5,168		N/A	35,669	644	2,398	302	235,909	13,768
Ecuador	31,881		1,569		3,433	26,879	159	1,807	89	80,171	4,544

The origin of the virus is China. Whether it is a synthetic virus developed in the country's laboratories or it is a case of transmission from other living beings to humans is yet to be ascertained. But if current debates and claims by researchers and logic providers are to be believed, then it seems that the Covid-19 virus originated from the horrible eating of all sorts of animals, birds and reptiles by the Chinese. If the virus was synthesized in the laboratories, as many are conjecturing it to be, then it represents a sadder state of affairs. In either of the possibilities, the fact remains that we humans have gone too far to challenge the delicate balance of Mother Earth and the natural environment. As a result, today, the entire human race has forced itself into a period of lockdown, quarantine and isolation. Despite having all the means, no one is able to go for a morning walk, go to the workplace, or travel by automobiles, trains, ships or aeroplanes. The entire fleet of buses, trains, limousines, cars, ships and aeroplanes are kept parked in an immobile condition.

The Corona virus disease is wreaking havoc across the world and there is no clarity on how long it will last. The full extent of the damage, both economic and non-economic, may not be known for a while. However, it is possible to draw some important lessons and underline the key trends in a post-Covid-19 world.

Ecosystem as a sink

There is no certainty as to when normalcy of human life will return on the face of the earth. It is not clear whether mankind will be able to step out of their houses without a face mask. There is a huge doubt over whether the entire workforce will return to their workplaces in the near future (in the next couple of years). It is not certain whether the hospitality and tourism industry will ever return to the pre-November 2019 era. Maybe we humans have irreversibly changed the freedom of movement and travel for many years to come. These are the results of human ego and efforts to show off human supremacy over nature. We consciously need to analyze and change our thinking to bring back normalcy, even though it appears to be a distant dream now.

Design thinking is important to keep human life going on the earth. Let us deliberate on some of the most vital issues and mistakes that we carried out in the past, so as to step into this current difficult situation.

Reckless mining

Mining and exploration of natural resources is necessary for economic development. One of the most important prerequisites before commencement of activities in mining is environmental impact assessment. While most of the mining industries carry out due diligence, there are instances where impact assessment is ignored. We often hear news of illegal mining and unlawful activities on river bed sand in different parts of the world.

Unnecessary comfort

The prolific use of natural resources to provide comfort beyond the real need has given rise to activities that have disturbed the delicate balance of the natural environment.

Some of these activities are:

a. felling of trees for construction activities,
b. use of chemicals for agriculture and non-biodegradable material manufacture, and
c. use of non-biodegradable materials.

All these are to satisfy factors such as:

i.   profligacy in consumption,
ii.   greed rather than need,
iii. deforestation, and
iv.   huge vehicles for commuting inside the cities.

City planning and human population

Concentration of human population in cities has given rise to problems such as emission of exhaust gases from a large number of vehicles and increase in ambient temperature The formation of the atmosphere as a sink for emitted pollutants have given rise to a grave environmental impact.

Population explosion

The rise in population in some countries, due to ignorance of its impact on society, economy and natural resources, is another prime reason for environmental pollution.

Environmental impact

The combined effect of all these factors, and many more that we have not been able to enumerate here, have given rise to immediate consequences such as the following.

- **Inversion temperature**

Ours is a simple citizen's life. So, let us have a simple understanding of complex scientific phenomena. Though a basic understanding of real and ideal gases, adiabatic expansion, and Joule Thomson effects is necessary, for the time being let us understand only gases and atmospheric temperature. Let us, for a while, restrict our understanding to the fact that gases expand when heated and cool when they are passed through a constricted aperture.

So, in normal atmospheric conditions, away from industrial effects and vehicular pollution, hot air remains on the top portion while cool air remains closer to the earth's troposphere. Following this natural law, the generated gases containing pollutants like oxides of sulphur and nitrogen, smoke and particulate matter in the industrial areas move to the top portion of the stratosphere, and the lower strata is clean.

But under certain conditions, this phenomenon changes form. The emitted gases, smoke and particulates do not get any way to escape to the top strata and they get accumulated in the lower strata. This condition is known as 'inversion temperature'. That means people and all other living beings start breathing polluted air. They get suffocated initially, followed by respiratory diseases and death, in more acute cases.

If this inversion temperature takes place in winter (when there is fog), then smoke and fog form a thick blanket of poisonous gases known as smog (smoke + fog). Most of the environmental disasters with respect to air pollution have occurred because of smog. Some well-known but painful incidents are Donora smog in 1948 and London smog in 1952.

Unfortunately, instances of smog are not part of history. Smog has spread and it is a common occurrence in most cities of the world. You and I can encounter smog even in smaller cities. Vehicular exhaust, industrial emissions, construction activities, and mining have made smog almost a common occurrence. As a result, respiratory diseases are on the rise.

- **Dust in Brownian motion**

The atmosphere is used as a natural sink for all forms of pollutants, including dust and particulate materials. Billions of tonnes of coal, metalliferous, non-metaliferrous materials, and petroleum products are processed, on our planet. They contribute to dust in the air. Other sources of dust include exhaust from engines and worn-out tyres from transportation facilities.

These dust particles keep floating in the atmosphere like Brownian movements of particles. Apart from health hazards, dust and particulates also cause fluctuations in the pH level of rainwater. Pure rain drops precipitate on the surface of the earth as acid rain.

- **Acid rain**

Rainfall usually serves as a cleansing agent for the atmosphere, removing soluble gases, suspended particulate matter, and other atmospheric pollutants. However, due to the presence of these matter in the atmosphere, rainwater gets contaminated by the cleansing process mentioned above. Oxides of nitrates and sulphur from gaseous emissions come in contact with rain drops, and sulphuric and nitric acids are formed. These acids bring down the pH level of rainwater and cause acid rain.

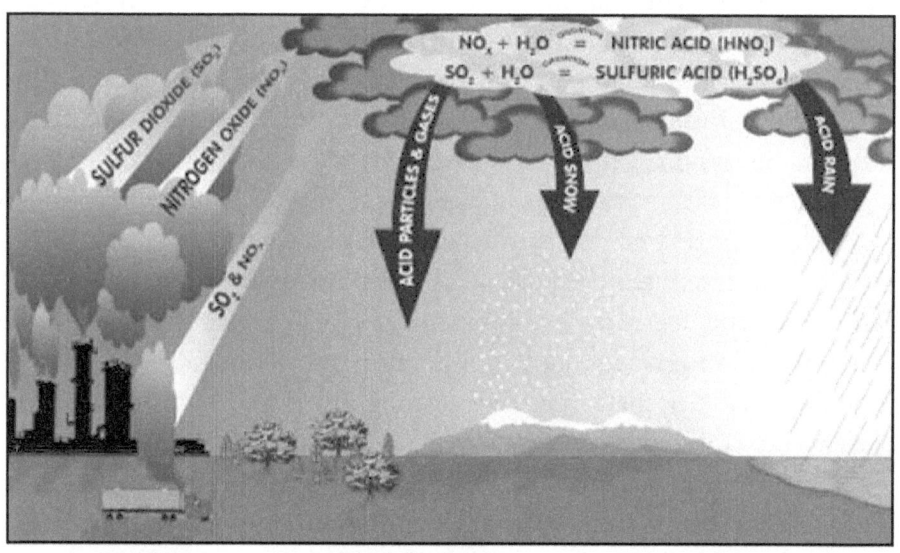

The presence of dissolved solids and metallic matter is an indication that rainwater is polluted. Sometimes, the concentrations of certain metals exceed the standards of safe drinking water in some countries.

Burning of coal, furnace oil, diesel oil, engine oil and petrol produce a large amount of SO2 (sulphur dioxide), which is released in the atmosphere. SO2 thus liberated into the atmosphere reacts photochemically or catalytically with other atmospheric contaminants, forming sulphuric acid.

Photochemically, the reaction may proceed as:

$$SO2 + hv \text{ (photon)} \rightarrow SO_2^* \text{ (excited)} \tag{1}$$
$$SO_2^* + O_2 \rightarrow SO_4^* \tag{2}$$
$$SO_4^* + O_2 \rightarrow SO_3 + O_3 \tag{3}$$
$$H_2O + SO_3 \rightarrow H_2SO_4 \tag{4}$$

and catalytically, it may proceed as:

$$SO_2 + O_2 \rightarrow SO_3 \tag{5}$$
$$SO_3 + H_2O \rightarrow H_2SO_4 \tag{6}$$

Design thinking in environmental management

The natural environment is very large and complex. It consists of the earth's crust, the surrounding atmosphere, and the various forms of life that exist in the zone between 600 m above and 10,000 m below sea level. It is humanly difficult to bring back the natural environment to a stage where it was pure and serene. Mankind in every age has exploited the natural environment and brought it to a very difficult stage. Reversing from this stage will involve the sum total of many corrective stages by: (a) individuals, (b) individual activities, (c) groups, and (d) group activities. It is a job to be completed by the human race in totality and with synergy. We shall need some design thinking in these noble activities.

Afforestation

Afforestation is the process of planting trees, or sowing seeds, in a barren land devoid of any trees to create a forest. The term should not be confused with reforestation, which is the process of specifically planting native trees into a forest that has a decreasing number of trees. Reforestation refers to planting trees on land that was previously a forest whereas afforestation refers to planting trees on patches of land that were not previously covered by forests.

It is well-known that afforestation can have many positive effects on degraded land, including conservation of soil on degraded land by reducing soil erosion as well as increasing soil organic matter, improving soil structure, sequestering carbon, increasing nutrient cycling, and providing wildlife habitat.

Afforestation also increases water resources for agricultural activities. It helps to improve the quality of air. Afforestation also helps in dealing with global warming. Trees help to maintain a proper balance between oxygen and carbon dioxide in the atmosphere.

The major advantages of afforestation are:

1. Constant supply of forest products
2. Prevention of soil erosion
3. Stabilization of climate
4. Reversing global warming and climate change
5. Better quality of air
6. Improved watershed
7. Preservation of wildlife
8. Provision of employment and economic opportunities

One of the authors of this book, Manoj Kumar Patel, has carried out climatological changes and meteorological changes in the city of Rourkela (the industrial capital of the state of Odisha in India) by analyzing data on temperature, rainfall and potential evapotranspiration for a period from 1968 to 1989. The study showed the following areas of concern.

1. The study area is gradually getting into semi-arid climate from its earlier sub-humid climate. It is a point of concern.
2. The number of droughts during the first decade i.e. during 1968 to 1978 was 5. During the second decade, i.e. during 1979 to 1989, there were 6 droughts.
3. The number of severe droughts in the first decade was 2 (1972 and 1976). The number of severe droughts during the second decade was 3 (1979, 1985 and 1989).
4. The frequency in the number of droughts was also found to be in the second decade.

These were the results of design thinking, which involved steps, experiments and calculations.

In view of the importance of ambient temperature and rainfall in determining the weather and climate of an area, the following parameters can be studied with respect to some relevant techniques.

1. Potential evapotranspiration (PET) calculation
2. Aridity index determination
3. Moisture index determination
4. Humidity index determination
5. Water balance method
6. Method of least square
7. Asymmetry
8. Inter-annual variability

Each of the above mentioned stages were completed with these basic steps:
(a) empathise (b) define (c) ideate (d) prototype (e) test

The climatic conditions of any region can be found out by analyzing simple raw data on daily ambient temperature, humidity and rainfall. Similar studies with refined design thinking ought to be carried out before projects on industries, cities, mining, dams and reservoirs are approved by governments.

Thus, data analysis through design thinking is a very important aspect. It helps in understanding the natural environment. It subsequently prompts mankind (policy-makers) to take corrective actions to make the earth a habitable place now and forever.

A few of the outcomes from studies like this are seen in mankind's progress towards adopting (a) electric vehicles in lieu of diesel and petrol vehicles, (b) harnessing solar, tidal and wind power in place of fossil fuel fuels, (c) green technologies, (d) biodegradable materials, and so on.

Environmental impact assessment

Ishikawa Diagram, Fish Bone Diagram, and Root Cause Analysis are different names for the same activity of finding out the root cause of a problem. The activity finds the root cause and then eliminates it, so that it does not recur. The cause-effect analysis is another technique to understand the impact of any act.

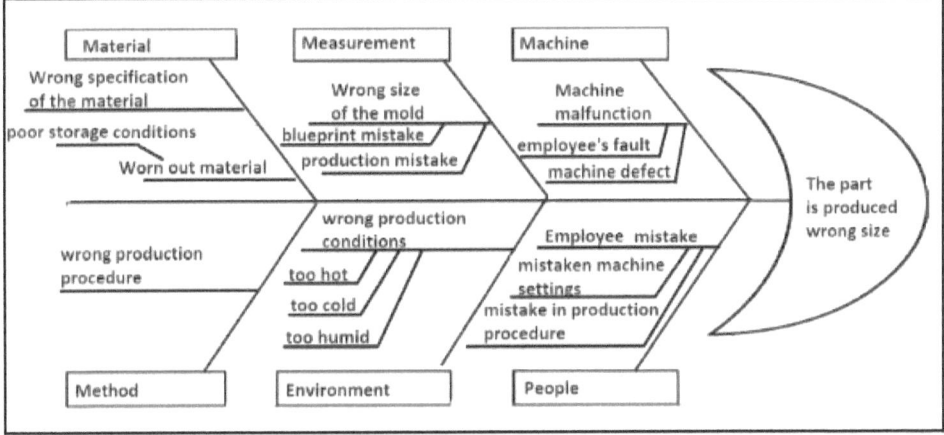

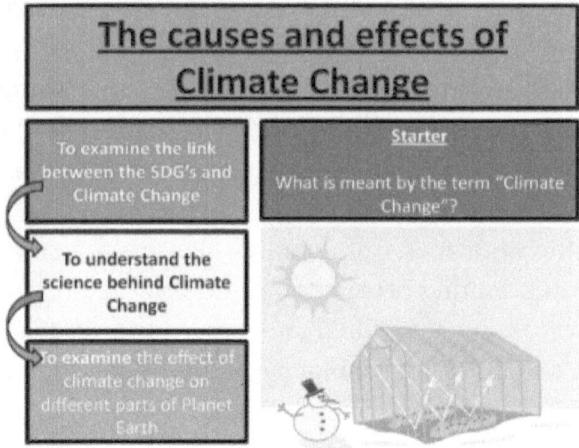

Root Cause Analysis is used in the subject of environmental studies. It is called Environmental Impact Assessment or EIA. Impact assessment is not a straightjacket approach. The exact procedures followed in carrying out EIA are by no means simple and/or straightforward, as many different projects are proposed for the numerous and varied environmental situations. Many attempts have been made in the past in this direction, and a review of these efforts shows that there are five factors of impact appraisal, which must be considered in an EIA study. These five basic factors are as follows:

1. Identification
2. Measurement
3. Interpretation
4. Communication
5. Monitoring

EIA employs different procedures for different activities. For example, the assessment method used in the construction of a highway is different from the one applied in the case of the mining industry. Design thinking comes into play to find out the best suited EIA.

The different EIA methodologies are:

1. Ad hoc methods
2. Checklists
3. Matrices
4. Overlays

5. Networks
6. Quantitative or Index methods
7. Systems models

One of the EIA methods developed for assessment of impact in industrial cities and mining areas has been devised by Manoj Kumar Patel. A brief description of the method has been given here for immediate reference by the reader.

The technique developed is an improvement of the method prescribed by Leopold et al, which was highly subjective. In our method, an attempt has been made to make the environmental degradation evaluation technique quantitative to a certain extent. The approach for environmental assessment entails the use of a number of assessment tools to quantify the ranking number from 1 to 10, as used in Leopold matrices. The environmental attributes, mathematical formulae and assumptions to give the attribute impact value for environmental degradation in proposed matrices are briefly described in the subsequent paragraphs:

1. Environmental attributes
2. Environmental parameters
3. Theoretical assumptions
4. Mathematical calculations

The outcomes are fairly precise and the suggestions are implementable.

Natural dust trappers

About 28 years ago, the author (Manoj Kumar Patel) and his research guide, Dr Tej Narayan Tiwari, had done some fundamental research on design thinking in the area of 'role of trees in mitigating dust pollution in the atmosphere'. Now, in the context of writing this chapter, it has come as a reminder to the authors of this book to deliberate on the same issue. The references in scientific journals where the work appeared are: Tiwari, T.N. and Patel, M.K. 1993. Effect of cement dust on some plants: Correlations among foliar dust deposition, chlorophyll content and calcium content. Ind. J. Envt. Prot. 13 (2): 93 – 95; and, Patel, M.K. and Tiwari, T.N. 1991. A study of dust pollution in the Rourkela industrial complex. Part – I. Ind. J. Proc. 11: 29 – 31.

These are testimonies to the assumption made 30 years ago that we need to have more trees to combat air pollution and keep the air on earth breathable for our posterity. But what we are observing as citizens of the world is that our next generation is now going out with masks over their nose and mouth. We are seeing morning walkers with face masks. So, in every sense, we have polluted the air in our only life-sustaining planet and made the air hard to breathe. Maybe in another 30 years, we will make it totally unbreathable.

Conclusion

Humans constitute a miniscule of the potential in front of nature. But damages caused in different parts of the world in the form of chemicals manufacturing, nuclear ammunition, nuclear tests, biological research, deforestation, construction of ultra-mega mines, metal processing industries, and huge power plants, large-scale water transfers, and jungle fires know no bounds and political boundaries. Emissions of radiation from nuclear power plants and toxic gases from chimneys and processes of process plants travel beyond the borders of origin countries and affect millions of innocent people even in far-off countries. The pollution generated moves across the globe through air, water and radiations. Thus, moral responsibilities are the only solution to this global problem.

So, each one of us needs to vouch for making tiny contributions to minimize wastes on our ecosystem by:

a. making use of required natural resources like water, food and land,
b. using public transport system for commuting,
c. having patience to sit at home with family members and avoid going out unnecessarily,
d. using our ACs less – by at least 2 hours every day,
e. planting at least 12 trees in a year,
f. felling no trees in our lifetime,
g. supporting sustainable development efforts of governments,
h. rationing fuels,
i. reducing use of cars and bikes,
j. using green fuels,
k. using green firecrackers,
l. using bicycles for short distance commuting, and so on.

It is also absolutely necessary for the thinktanks and planning commissions set up by governments to plan and ensure the following:

a. shifting of industries to less densely populated places,
b. restricting city sizes by correlating availability of natural resources like surface and groundwater with population growth over a period of time, say centuries,

c.   building of new cities,
d.   planning sustainable large-scale water transfers, and
e.   last but the most important: population control.

Synergy effects from these activities will go a long way in contributing to the healthy growth of living beings and a clean natural environment for a long time.

Each one of us is a stakeholder on this earth and each of us has to 'design think' to save the earth from misuse and damage. So that the morning walk in a densely populated industrial city with heavy traffic doesn't turn into a death trap. The spread of the menace of environmental pollutants will travel faster than we can think of. Design thinking will be the saviour.

03

Design Thinking in Mining Industry

Introduction

Before finding the applicability and uses of DT in mining operations, we need to have some fundamental clarity about mining. Precious metals, minerals, oils and gases are available below the surface of the earth. These resources are taken out by means of digging the earth's surface. The process of digging is called excavation and mining. For the sake of simplicity in understanding, we shall use the word 'mining' in this chapter to refer to this process.

There are two major types of techniques applied in mining activities. These two techniques are surface mining and sub-surface/underground mining.

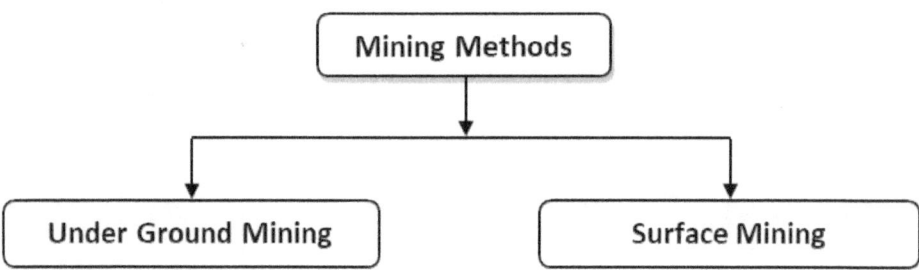

Mining per se is a highly complex and tough method. It calls for excellent skills beyond theoretical knowledge. It involves precise as well as monster-size machinery round the clock. Mining activities deal with natural forces and are laden with hazards and life risks. There is nothing easy in mining activities, but from a few specific points of view, surface or open cast mining is a little less cumbersome and less hazardous compared to underground mining operations.

A couple of photographs of surface mining and underground mining are given here for reference and to appreciate the complexity of the operations both on the surface and beneath the surface of Mother Earth.

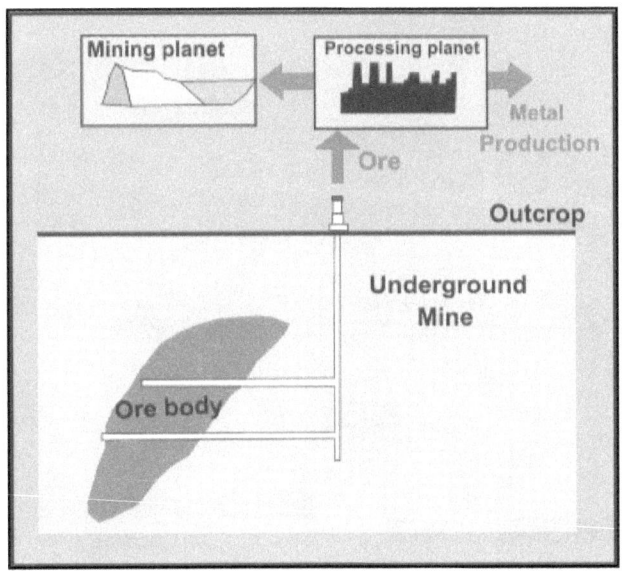

By Mining Method

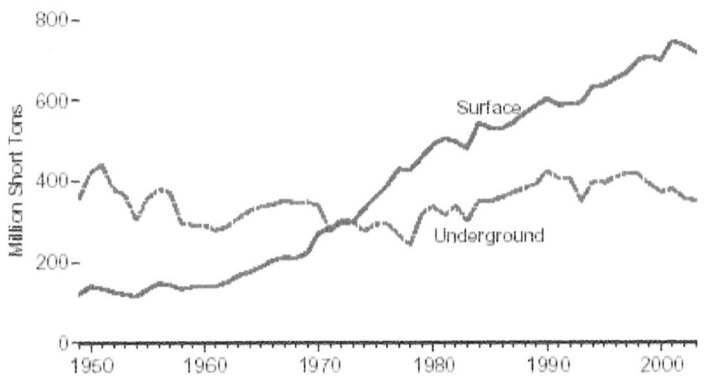

Source: Energy Information Administration

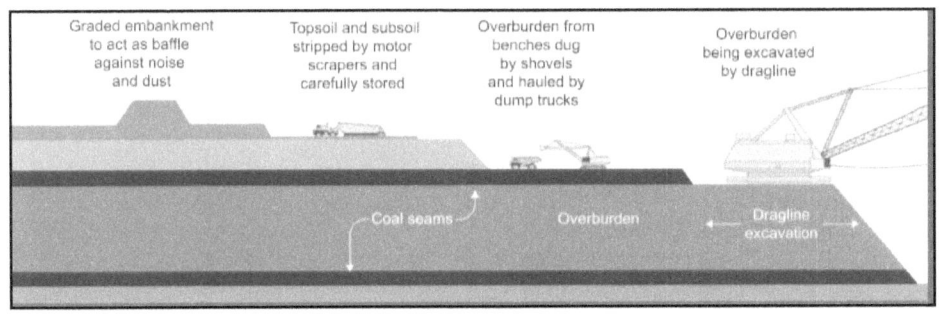

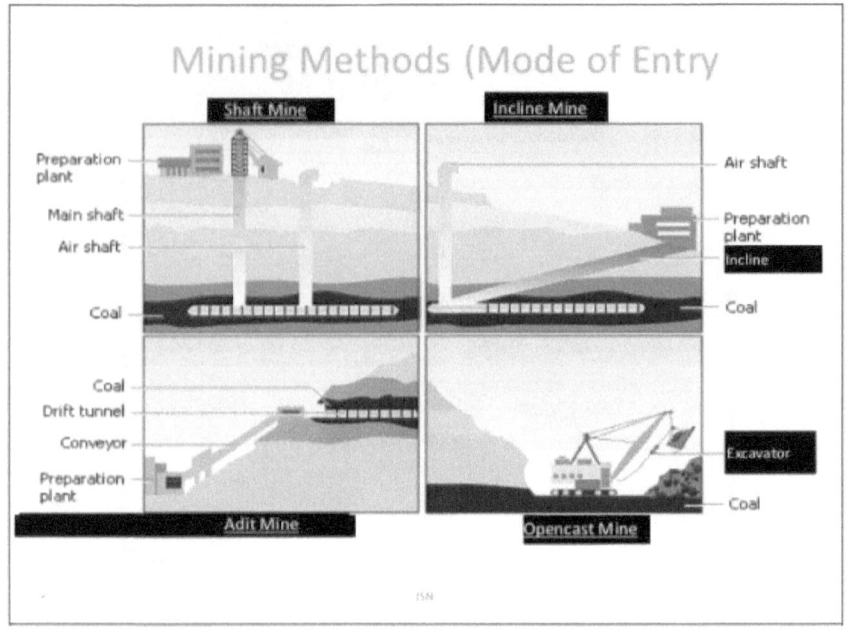

Underground mining

Underground mining 01

Underground mining 02

Underground mining 03

Underground mining 04

Surface or opencast mining

Surface mining 01

Surface mining 02

Surface mining 03

Surface mining 04

There are a few more operations that involve identical or near-identical operations such as tunnelling, large-scale water transfers, construction of roads in difficult terrains, construction of bridges, and demolition of old and abandoned structures for safety, security and generation of space for better utilization of land. We will cover these areas in the subsequent sections of this chapter.

Tunnelling and Road construction

Tunnelling 01

Tunnelling 02

Tunnelling 03

Planned demolition

Constructive demolition 01

Constructive demolition 02

Constructive demolition 03

Large-scale water Transfer

Large-scale water transfer 01

Large-scale water transfer 02

Large-scale water transfer 03

Large-scale water transfer 04

Large-scale water transfer 05

Large-scale water transfer 06

Large-scale water transfer 07

The earliest known mine for a specific mineral is a coal mine from southern Africa, which appeared 40,000 to 20,000 years ago. But mining did not become a significant industry until more advanced civilizations developed about 10,000 to 7,000 years ago. In early times, the only metals available were those found in a metallic state in nature. The most abundant one was copper. But gold, silver and mercury were also found and prized. The application of fire to excavate materials became a technological breakthrough and proved to be one of the most critical advancements of civilization. In fact, excavated elements transformed with the application of heat. As a result, pottery hardened to last more than a season. Metals could be melted and formed into objects.

During the rise of Europe, governments gave miners extensive rights to take land and profit from the minerals they found in it. Nevertheless, the governments always required a portion of the revenue from mining as payment for granting mining rights. As a result, the realization dawned, and endured that countries could not develop without the exploitation of natural resources. Civilization progressed, thus necessitating an increasing amount of mined material to manufacture the needs of everyday life and fund the economies of nations. The influx of this mineral wealth from the New World financed the Renaissance. Eventually, the creation and expansion of countries in the New World, along with the development of the Industrial Age, resulted in the generation of the mining industry that we have today.

Egyptians and Sumerians smelted gold and silver from ore 6,000 years ago. As a result, these metals began to have a value that was transferable between people and cultures. Approximately 5,500 years ago, in the history of mining, came the discovery of tin.

The General Mining Act of 1872 intended and succeeded at establishing and maintaining our present level of civilization. In fact, if humans had not put the structure in place to provide an incentive to prospectors and miners, our lives would probably have been entirely different. It was our industrial might (based on mined resources) that helped win several wars. It built the railroads and highways, bridges and cities. Ultimately, changes in the Mining Act of 1872 are necessary to make mining more compatible with our expanding population. But we should not forget, underestimate or lose the important lessons learnt in the history of mining to the modern life that we relish.

Mined resources will take us to the future. The growth of electronics has only increased the need for copper, the first metal used by humans. The construction of green energy resources (wind, solar, geothermal) requires extensive mined resources to provide lightweight aluminium and the special alloys necessary for new applications.

In the beginning of this section, we mentioned that mining is the extraction of valuable minerals and other geological materials from the earth, usually from an ore body, lode, vein, seam, and reef or placer deposit. Ores recovered by mining include metals, coal, oil shale, gemstones, limestone, chalk, dimension stone, rock salt, potash, gravel and clay. The three most common types of surface mining are open pit mining, strip mining, and quarrying.

Mined materials are needed to construct roads and hospitals, build automobiles and houses, make computers and satellites, generate electricity, and provide the many other goods and services that consumers enjoy. In addition, mining is economically important to producing regions and countries.

Mining is required to obtain any material that cannot be grown through agricultural processes or created artificially in a laboratory or factory.

The three major components of mining are exploration, mining and processing. After the mineral deposit has been identified through exploration, the industry makes a considerable investment in mine development before production begins.

The first step in the production stage is recovering the minerals. This is the process of extracting the ore from rocks using a variety of tools and machinery. The second step is processing. The recovered minerals are processed in huge crushers or mills to separate commercially valuable minerals from their ores.

Necessity is the mother of invention. Every now and then, miners and excavators in the field face challenges with respect to ease, safety and complexity. These are aspects that prompt the need for reassurance and solutions. Thus, design thinking is absolutely necessary in the field of mining. Miners all around the world will be benefitted by and thankful for real-life solutions to the problems they face perennially.

Very specifically, we shall now discuss design thinking in mining operations with respect to certain parameters: mining equipment, high-energy materials, materials used for mining, operating procedures, logistics, and conveyance.

Design Thinking in Mining

The sequence of operations in mining is surveying, drilling, energy materials, operations in use of energy materials, transportation of energy materials, blasting, excavation and then transportation of the excavated materials. We shall discuss application of design thinking in all these areas.

DT in Drilling and Blasting

Drilling and blasting are the two most significant operations that play a crucial role in the downstream stages. Drilling makes use of machinery like drilling machines. Drilling machines drill bore holes, the depth of which varies from 4 metres to 75 metres. The diameter of the holes varies from 25 mm to 375 mm.

The normal practice adopted for drilling involves carefully engineered blasting, which is an important aspect of successful open pit mining as:

(1) pits become deeper and steeper,

(2) there is a need for quality separation to avoid dilution and ore losses during blasting, and

(3) greater attention is paid to optimizing the entire mine-mill fragmentation system due to energy cost concerns.

It has been observed that operators pay more attention to blasting than drilling programmes. Meanwhile, it is crucial to consider both simultaneously to achieve an optimized design. Innovative efforts have been done by many researchers to improve efficiencies and reduce cost.

Works carried out by researchers were reported in an article titled *'Optimized design of drilling and blasting operations in open pit mines under technical and economic uncertainties by system dynamic modelling'*. A system dynamic method for modelling drilling and blasting operations was proposed in the article. This model could efficiently connect and evaluate all the technical, economic and environmental parameters of these operations. In addition, the changes in parameters through the simulation period (one year of production), especially in case of the total production and costs were measured. An optimization process for bit diameter in two different conditions—deterministic and uncertainty—was carried out. It was shown that the optimum result can be totally different in the case of deterministic and uncertainty conditions. In spite of assuming a normal density function in conditions of uncertainty for the parameters, the distribution of optimum bit diameters was more fitted to the generalized extreme values. In addition, the total drilling and blasting costs in the uncertainty conditions differ from \$9.475 million to \$10.020 million, which present higher costs compared to the deterministic optimization (\$9.402 million). It was also proposed that the real distribution function for the uncertain parameters could be defined by gathering the real data of a mine for running a more practical model.

In another work published in the article titled *New trends in drilling and blasting technology,* the researcher has discussed that unit operations such as drilling, blasting, excavation, loading, hauling and crushing are interrelated variables in the total cost equation. Development, advancement and utilization of innovative technologies are very important for the mining industry to be cost effective. In modern mines, it is very common to encounter the latest forms of laser measurement technologies, global positioning systems (GPS), communication technology and computer systems. The developments in the areas of planning and design of blasts, drill monitoring, drill hole deviation, drill machine navigation systems and laser profiling systems have been discussed in his paper. The innovative practices in the areas of bulk loading of explosives, controlled blasting, explosive performance measurement, and evaluation of blast outcome and productivity have been outlined. The role to be played by electronic detonators in the next millennium to improve blasting efficiency and mining economics has also been described.

In his the article titled *Recent Advancements in Drilling and Blasting*, the researcher has described the use of an adequate and reliable method in dealing with drilling and blasting operations to minimize the risk and optimize the operation in a safe manner. The improvement in performance of drilling and blasting has been described to be improved by embracing the latest technology, which is the common goal of all modern mining companies. This paper article dealt deals with the application of modern drilling and blasting technology such as GPS, laser technology, and CTC system (communication, techniques and computer).

For example, with the combination of a laser range finder and a face profiler, a single operator can accurately measure and record critical depth vs. burden data from a single location, improve efficiency, maximize job safety, and better control the blast design. It is crucial to combine all parameters, including selection of explosives, rock properties and surface blast design, to devise efficient and cost-effective blasting, which achieves the desired degrees of fragmentation.

Computer-aided blast design and test-blast practices have replaced trial-and-error methods, providing a controlled environment. Of course, any blast design is only as good as the data. For the most reliable data, designers need a couple of high-tech tools. Ideally, the blast would be designed with computer assistance using information from laser surveys, geotechnical information, and other data. The hole locations are placed on the blast plan maps. The final design is downloaded to the drill equipped with GPS capability. The drill machine can then drill the blast holes accurately on the designed locations.

The laser profiler provides a three-dimensional reading of the blast face to decide where to drill and load the explosives. The laser systems can also be used to survey the muck pile after blasting. The volume of the rock broken by shot can be obtained. The swell of the blasted material can also be determined. Swell is a measure of the looseness and, therefore, the diggability of the blast. Swell can be correlated to excavator productivity, and this information can be fed back into the blast design for use in designing subsequent blasts in the same area. Proper placement and loading of the front-row holes is absolutely essential for good blasting. The laser profiler helps the blasting group to design effective front-row blasthole locations and explosives loading requirements that reflect the actual conditions.

Another technology that has great importance for drilling accuracy and integration of drilling and blasting operations is GPS applied to drill positioning on individual blastholes. These systems allow the blast plan with blasthole locations to be downloaded to the drill. Some form of moving display is used to guide the drill onto the designed blasthole location. The drill can be positioned within one-third metre of the designed location.

Some systems provide for azimuth as well as coordinates so that the drill can be accurately located on angled holes. If the elevation coordinate is provided for, hole depths can be adjusted for variations in bench topography. Therefore, the drill can be accurately spotted without the need for extensive field surveying. Equally important is the fact that the systems record exactly where the hole is drilled. This is essential for data transfer to blasthole loading operations because it provides the way to access hole depth and rock strength profile information in the monitoring database.

Until recently, the assessment of blasting results had been subjective and thus it was neither accurate and nor not impartial. To properly assess the results achieved, quantitative data can now be obtained at the face. Several mines are using computer-based fragmentation analysis. The technique can be used for assessing blasted material, dumper, and crusher station. There are techniques available to predict fragmentation from a particular blast design. Methods like Kuz-Ram, in software form, predict fragmentation size distribution. This can be used for optimizing explosives, patterns or other design changes.

The article *Innovative developments in drilling and blasting techniques for rapid excavation of drivages in mines* says that, in time-bound mega construction projects of four to five years, modern methods of rapid tunnel driving are being considered as the only solution to achieve a high rate of progress. We now have bigger and faster drill machines and excavators. In explosives technology too, significant progress has been made towards having safer explosives and accurate initiating systems, which have increased the overall control over blasting in terms of vibration, fragmentation, throw of the blasted muck pile, and overall blast economics. The developments have been mainly done in automation and precise drilling techniques. These include automation of the drill rigs and improved design of bits, rods, bit inserts, and bailing systems. Underground blasting in India has traditionally been done with packaged explosives. Though packaged explosives have served the industry for decades, they possess the problems of safety hazards, slow charging, manual handling, no product flexibility, and partial energy utilization due to decoupling. This had compelled blasting engineers and researchers of the eighties to initiate a thought process in search of a system that would lead to a paradigm shift in underground blasting technology. In the late eighties, a few explosives manufacturers came up with charging systems for underground use. These systems had the inherent advantages of pumped emulsion explosives, such as speed and safety, besides introducing the concept of product flexibility. Product flexibility leads to a greater rate of advance and lower damage at the back for better roof stability. The electronic detonators specifically designed for tunnelling provide the accuracy and flexibility of electronic timing, at a reasonable price, with rapid and easy operations at the tunnel face. Researchers and authors of the said paper have discussed the latest developments that have taken place in explosives—initiating systems and drilling technology for tunnelling at a few tunnelling and cavern excavation sites for enhanced rate of excavation.

Newly designed tools and drill bits have been manufactured by many companies to ease drilling and blasting at a lesser cost and time. Some of the drilling products are Rotary drilling tool bits Expandera, Rotary drilling bit subs, Rotary drilling stabilizers, Rotary drilling deck bushings and Rotary drilling pipes.

The global mining drill bits market size was valued at $1,145,000 thousand in 2018. It is projected to reach $1,711,800 thousand by 2026, growing at a CAGR of 5.1% from 2019 to 2026. Mining drill bits are utilized to drill or dig the earth's surface for mining operations. These drill bits are also used to dig holes in stones or rocks for mining. Mining drill bits include Rotary drill bits and DTH hammers bits. Drill bits come in different sizes—from bits less than 150 mm to those more than 300 mm. In addition, these drills are used to drill holes in the earth's surface to place the explosives for blasting.

Players in the mining industry are investing heavily in expanding their capacity to meet the increase in demand for metals and ores, owing to the growth of the automotive sector. For instance, in 2018, Atlas Copco acquired two companies, Renegade Drilling Supplies Proprietary Ltd and Hy-Performance Fluid Power Pvt. Ltd., an Australian service provider for mining and infrastructure, to expand its product portfolio of drilling consumables for mining exploration. Moreover, due to the rise in the consumption of natural resources by China's huge population, the sales in China's mining drill bits market increased progressively every year.

Technological innovations will support the growth of the mining drill bits market in the coming years. Artificial intelligence (AI) and machine learning will help mining companies to discover minerals for extraction, which is a critical process in the mining operation. AI can also facilitate high machine intelligence to generate precise blast holes, which is important for performing the blasting operation. IBM started the implementation of AI in its mining and drilling machines. These technology factors are anticipated to provide lucrative opportunities for the growth of the mining drill bits market in the coming years.

DT in mining process

There are many processes such as stemming, air spaces, and storage constraints where design thinking has helped in safety and productivity of mining operations. This is a specialized area, and we shall discuss the general aspects of it with a view to appreciate the applications.

Stemming with stem plugs

The efficiency of rock breaking goes up with the containment of evolved gases from the explosion for a longer time. Here the time is measured in the unit of 'milli seconds'. Stem plugs have been designed by many organizations to help miners to improve their productivity.

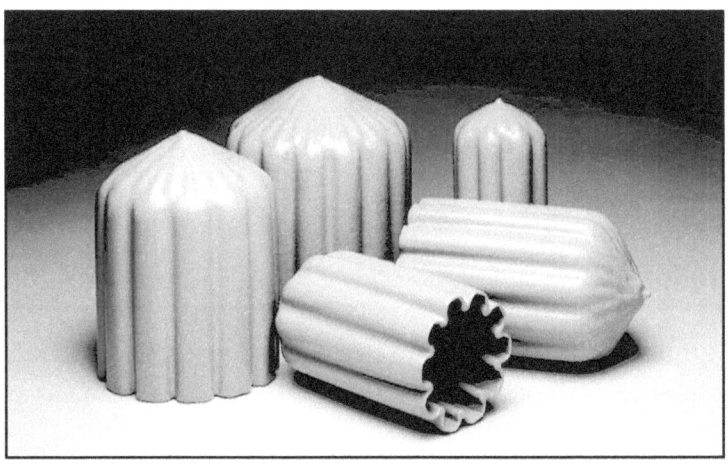

Self-inflating Gas Bags

Presence of gases in energy materials makes the rock blasting operation extremely powerful. But containing the gases is a cumbersome task. This cumbersome task has been made simple by the use of self-inflating gasbags.

As a rule of thumb, the savings in cost by use of gas bags are high.

No.	Description	UoM	Savings per metre of blast hole by using gasbags					
			83 mm	125 mm	160 mm	260 mm	310 mm	350 mm
01	Savings/metre of blast holes charged with gasbags	INR/ metre	120	299	502	1409	2007	2541

Gas bags are amazingly effective and cost competitive, if properly used with suitable explosives, especially in presplit and deep dragline benches.

Other Products

There are products like taggants and electronic accessories that are emerging in mining and excavation activities. Most of these are in the nascent stage.

But the concepts of design thinking and innovations, especially with respect to safety and security, are coming up with promising accuracy. We shall discuss these materials up to the present level and leave it to the researchers to complete the topic before we take up these as case studies.

DT in energy materials

Mechanical energy is used to break rocks with the help of chemicals. Chemical energy is converted into mechanical energy, which displaces rock from its stable and static positions. In general, energy materials are chemicals such as inorganic nitrates, nitro compounds, chlorates and perchlorates. Infinite numbers of combinations are used by mixing chemicals to get the desired energy from them. This is an indicative list of branded energy materials: Powergel, Aquadyne, Vijayblast, REL 6373, Emulboost, Primacord and Raydet. Thesey are manufactured by companies such as cDET, Solar Industries, GOCL Corporation Limited, and IDL Industries Limited.

The mining industry is diverse by nature. Different mines deal with different minerals such as coal, dolomite, granite, sandstone and shale. Different energy materials are required to break different types of rocks. Breaking up of sandstone requires different energy materials than what is required for breaking up other minerals such as coal, iron and dolomite. Thus, energy materials are unique and use-specific in nature. In common parlance, they are like medicines that are disease-specific and age(of patient)-specific.

Design thinking is absolutely necessary for energy materials. An energy material is basically a chemical or a mixture of chemicals, which, under the impact of an external source of energy like electrical, shock or mechanical energy, undergoes a simultaneous oxidation reduction reaction and generates a huge amount of heat and gases in split second of time. Different energy materials are used for different operations such as open cast mining, underground gassy mines, underground metal mines, tunnelling, rock blasting, planned demolitions, and construction of roads and bridges.

There are many parameters that can help in designing proper energy materials for a particular purpose. In simple terms, tailor-made energy materials can be designed. Variations can be made, in the type of input chemicals, the percentage of input chemicals, the process conditions, the density of energy materials, and so on. Changes in these parameters can largely change the output parameters such as heat energy and gaseous energy, both of which are manifestation of the input parameters.

Heat content or enthalpy is one such important parameter. There are several known laboratory and theoretical methods by which measures of enthalpy can be done. Use of bomb calorimeter is one such experimental method. Another theoretical method is determination of enthalpy of each ingredient used in the formulations. For example, the theoretical calculation of the heat aenergy of ammonium nitrate diesel oil (ANFO) is 917 kcal/kg. Bomb calorimeter also shows the same value i.e. 900 – 930 kcal/kg for ANFO. When the same experiment is carried out with different percentages of input materials in the basic ANFO formulation, then both the theoretical and calorimeter values match with negligible difference, may be due to some experimental error in using the calorimeter.

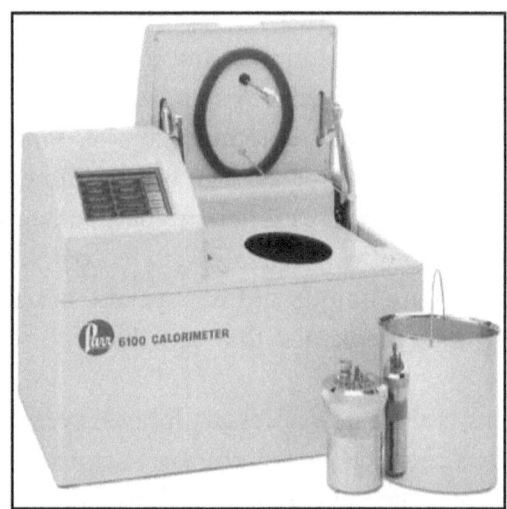

There are theoretical models such as BKW FORTRAN, CHEETAH and RUBY that can determine enthalpy content. Most of these models have been available for a long time for users. However, these are complex in nature and not available at an affordable licence cost. So, design thinking was applied to this area of need with the aim of debottlenecking the cost and user difficulty aspects. One of this book's authors, Manoj Kumar Patel, and his associates worked on this with views from newer perspectives and developed an energy calculation formula called GPeng. Values obtained through GPeng can be compared with the values obtained in the calorimeter. Both the values would match in each formulation that is tested. Other thermodynamic and thermochemistry parameters such as entropy, Gibbs free energy, volume expansion, oxygen factor, strength factor, RWS, ABS and RBS can be obtained by using GPeng.

Large numbers of parameters are used to form a regression analysis from which designing of proper energy material is made for a particular type of rock.

Manufacturers of energy materials and mining and blasting engineers use this model to design proper energy materials. This model has helped in the optimization of energy materials in terms of cost and quality in totality.

No	Output Parameter from GPeng	UoM
01	OF (oxygen balance factor)	No
02	SF (strength factor)	No
03	del H (enthalpy)	Kcal/kg
04	So (entropy)	Cal
05	Gibbs free energy	Kcal/kg
06	Volume expansion considering water is gas	Percent
07	Volume expansion considering water is liquid	Percent
08	Mole of oxygen generated from decomposition of OB	Mole/kg of product
09	Mole of oxygen required for complete combustion of FB	Mole/kg of product
10	Mole of gases generated from OB	Mole/kg of product
11	Mole of gases generated from FB	Mole/kg of product
12	Mole of gases generated from composition	Mole/kg of product
13	Absolute bulk strength or ABS	Kcal/cubic metre
14	Absolute weight strength (i.e. del H)	Kcal/kg
15	Relative bulk strength wrt ANFO or RBS_ANFO	Percent
16	Relative weight strength wrt ANFO or RWS_ANFO	Percent
17	Relative bulk strength wrt NG or RBS_NG	Percent
18	Relative weight strength wrt NG or RWS_NG	Percent

Sl. No.	Subject of Comparison	Experimental Method	Theoretical Method	Remarks
01	No Number of parameters that can be determined	7(Primary = 01 and Deduced = 06)	18 (Primary = 12 and Deduced = 06)	GPeng is better
02	Result precision	**Excellent**	with 95% Confidence level	Parr 6100 is better
03	Safety hazards	Hazard exists	No Hazard	GPeng is better
04	Statutory issues	Hazard exists	No Statutory Issues	GPeng is better
05	Statutory permission required from explosives department	Yes Permission required	No Not Required	GPeng is better
06	Cost	**High**	Less (25% of Experimental Method)	GPeng is better

The subject is of interest but we shall conclude here by saying that design thinking has given rise to reduction in cost and improvement in performances and productivity in mines.

DT in detonators

Detonators are used in mines to blast rocks. These are highly powerful and sensitive materials. Due to their sensitivity to shock, friction and electricity, these materials are chosen by anti-social elements. The safety and security of personnel and civilians are of utmost importance to all the nations of the world. So, world leaders are looking for a detonator that can be safe and secure even when anti-social elements lay their hands on it.

Design thinking has been able to provide a solution in this important area. Through design thinking, scientists have been able to develop detonators that are password protected. In the absence of the password, the detonator works like a regular piece of chalk. Detonators of this type are known as non-electric detonators, nonel detonators, or electronic detonators. To quench the curiosity of students, a few pictures of these detonators are given below.

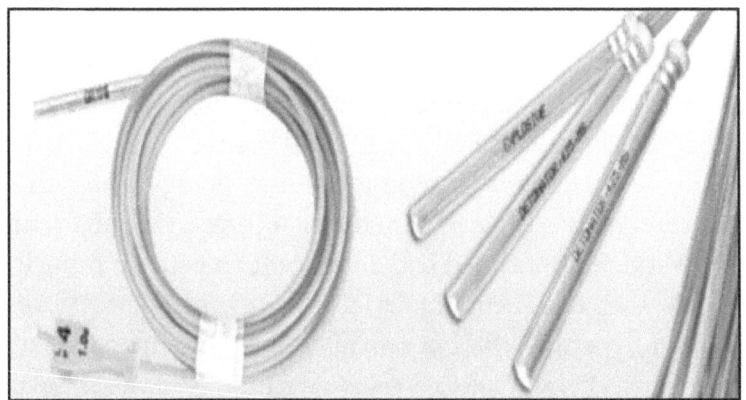

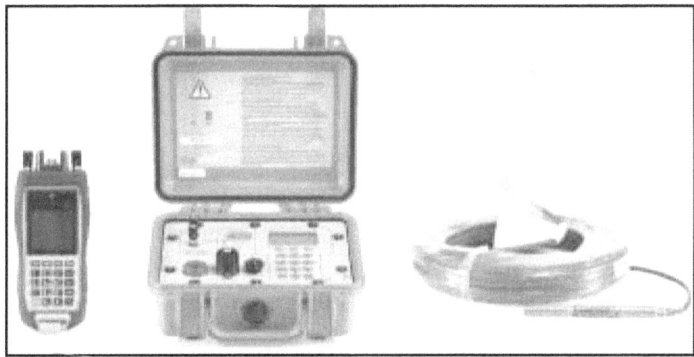

Conclusion

The topics around design thinking and mining are of so much interest that it is difficult to conclude these subjects within a few limited pages. However, the purpose of this particular chapter was to bring awareness among students that the subject area of design thinking is so pervasive that it can be applied to the allied areas of mining and high-energy materials.

The authors can visualize that, in the near future, the subject of mining will get more and more inclined and dependent on better mining processes in drilling, blasting and energy materials. Energy materials are soon going to see a phase full of powerful but safe materials from the points of view of manufacturing, usage, storage and transportation. A few of these products will be manufactured using eco-friendly energy materials and nonels, with in-built presence of taggants.

04

Design Thinking in Agriculture

Introduction

Back in 1960 in America, a revolutionary thinking was conceived by the American agricultural scientist Norman Ernest Borlaug. This thinking changed the way agriculture was seen and practised. This was the beginning of design thinking in agriculture in the world. This was the beginning of the Green Revolution.

The world's worst recorded food disaster occurred in 1943 in British-ruled India. Known as the Bengal Famine, an estimated 4 million people died of hunger that year in eastern India. Initially, this catastrophe was attributed to an acute shortfall in food production in the area. After independence, the scenario was going to worsen. That was the period when India evolved from various problems. Agriculture was one of the areas of evolution—in the form of Green Revolution.

The Green Revolution in India was a period when agricultural yield in the country increased due to improved agronomic technology. The revolution started in India in the early 1960s and led to an increase in food grain production, especially in Punjab, Haryana and Uttar Pradesh during the early phase. This initiative was undertaken by Mankombu Sambasivan Swaminathan, Father of Green Revolution in India.

A country in which 4 million people died in a year (1943) due to deficiency of food is now an exporter of food to many countries around the world. Now India has got so much surplus of food grains that it is planning to convert it into bio ethanol.

Despite industrial development, the basic need of life is fulfilled by agricultural products. When a country has food sufficiency, it is ever prepared to deal with setbacks in other areas. Thus, agriculture is given priority in developed and developing countries.

Norman Ernest Borlaug (25 March 1914 – 12 September 2009) was an American agricultural scientist and humanitarian. He is considered by some to be the father of modern agriculture and the father of Green Revolution. He won the 1970 Nobel Peace Prize for his lifetime's work. The mid-1960s was a very noteworthy period from the standpoint of agriculture. New high yielding varieties of wheat were developed by Prof. Borlaug and were adopted by a number of countries. Southern countries and Southeast Asia started adopting them on a wide scale. This new 'agricultural strategy' was termed a 'High Yielding Varieties Programme'.

TABLE 7.9. Progress in Foodgrains Production			*(million tonnes)*
Item	*1960-61*	*1980-81*	*2013-14*
Rice	35	54	106.5
Wheat	11	36	95.9
(*a*) Total cereals	69	119	245.5
(*b*) Total Pulses	13	11	19.3
(*c*) Total foodgrains (*a* + *b*)	82	130	264.8

The Green Revolution in India refers to a period when Indian agriculture was converted into an industrial system due to the adoption of modern methods and technology such as the use of high yielding variety seeds, tractors, irrigation facilities, pesticides and fertilizers.

The Green Revolution in India has given visible and remarkable results. It started in the 1960s. With the success of the revolution, India attained food self-sufficiency within a decade, by the end of the 1970s (first wave of the Green Revolution). The High Yielding Varieties Programme was constrained to only five crops—rice, wheat, jowar, maize and bajra.

Consequently, non – food grains were expelled from the domain of the new strategy. Wheat has stayed the bastion of Green Revolution over the years.

TABLE 7.10. Production of cash crops in India				
Items	1960-61	1970-71	1980-81	2013-2014
Sugarcane (m. tonnes)	110	126	134	350.0
Cotton (m. bales)	6	5	7	36.7
Jute & Mesta (m. bales)	4	6	8	11.6
Oilseeds (m. tonnes)	7	10	9	32.9

Centre permits conversion of surplus rice to ethanol for hand sanitisers

Move will lead to use of part of a stockpile of 30.57 million tonnes, which is almost 126% more than the buffer stock and strategic requirement norms

Shine Jacob & Sanjeeb Mukherjee | New Delhi
Last Updated at April 21, 2020 02:11 IST

ethanol from rice govt of India   ×   🎤

www.business-standard.com › Economy & Policy › News ▾
Centre permits conversion of surplus rice to ethanol for hand ...
1 day ago - The government on Monday allowed the conversion of surplus rice, available with the Food Corporation of India (FCI), to ethanol.
You visited this page on 20/4/20.

That is the power of design thinking. But what gave us relief for the last 60 years later gave us an adverse impact in terms of water availability. Groundwater and surface water was the lifeline of the Green Revolution but now the states of Punjab, Haryana, Uttar Pradesh and others are facing depletion of groundwater.

In order to sustain Green Revolution and high yield productions now, other possible aspects have to be looked into through newer visions. These newer visions will take birth from design thinking. If we look around, many such areas have already evolved. These new areas are evolving through design thinking in agriculture:

a.   high yield products
b.   water conservation
c.   crops requiring less water

d. soil nutrients
e. soil water retainers
f. biofertilizers
g. earthworm generating compost materials
h. wealth from wastes like coconut shells, banana peels and groundnut peels
i. nutraceuticals from grains
j. disease preventing spices like ginger, fenugreek, cumin seeds, garlic, turmeric and neem

Let us see what has been done so far and what best can be thought of through design thinking for future generations.

Soil water retainers

Mother Earth is thirsty, and the thirst has to be quenched during the travel from one season to the next. The earth needs water and moisture in order to nourish crop and vegetation on its lap. Water is life. Agriculture depends on water availability in time. Nearly 60% of India's agriculture depends on the rains.

Since 2015, India has been experiencing widespread drought conditions. In fact, around 600 million people in India are currently facing high-to-extreme water stress. Today, millions of farmers hit by drought and crop failure are struggling to stay alive. More than 80% of districts in the state of Karnataka and 70% in the state of Maharashtra have been declared drought affected. More than 6,000 tankers supply water to nearly 15,000 villages and hamlets in Maharashtra alone. According to the South Asia Drought Monitor, Tamil Nadu along with other Indian states such as Karnataka, Andhra Pradesh and Maharashtra are trapped in a severe dry cycle that has so far lasted six months.

India is the largest user of groundwater in the world. According to the government's report, by 2020, as many as 21 Indian cities could run out of groundwater, and, by 2030, nearly 40% of the country's population may have no access to drinking water. Groundwater, the source of 40% of India's water needs, is being depleted at an alarming rate. Water is becoming a serious economic issue for one of the world's largest economies. A study by the country's environment ministry found that desertification, land degradation, and drought cost India nearly 2.5% of GDP in 2014-15.

Water is necessary for agriculture. But it is gradually becoming scarce. This is true for groundwater as well as surface water.

While the government is doing its best to encourage people to hole, preserve and conserve water received from rain, it is also necessary for all citizens to think differently to find out ways to grow crops by using just the optimum amount of water. This is a wide area, and policies and procedures are necessary.

But we can reduce water consumption in our own way. If water use can be reduced in our kitchen gardens (villages have big kitchen gardens), flower plants in balconies (as seen in apartments, offices and malls), and vertical gardens that we see in the pillars of over bridges and metro railways, it would lead to preservation of water.

Entrepreneurs have developed such possibilities. They have thought of materials and procedures by thinking out of the box. This design thinking has given rise to more than one product that can be used as water retainers in the soil. That means presence or application of these materials will hold the moisture in the soil for a longer period. For example, if the water retention capacity of the soil is increased by 50%, the water requirement for the plants will come down by 50%.

Many great Innovative products have taken birth from design thinking. We shall discuss a couple of these such products here.

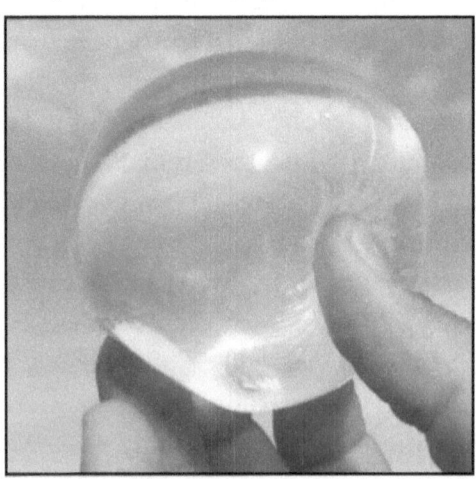

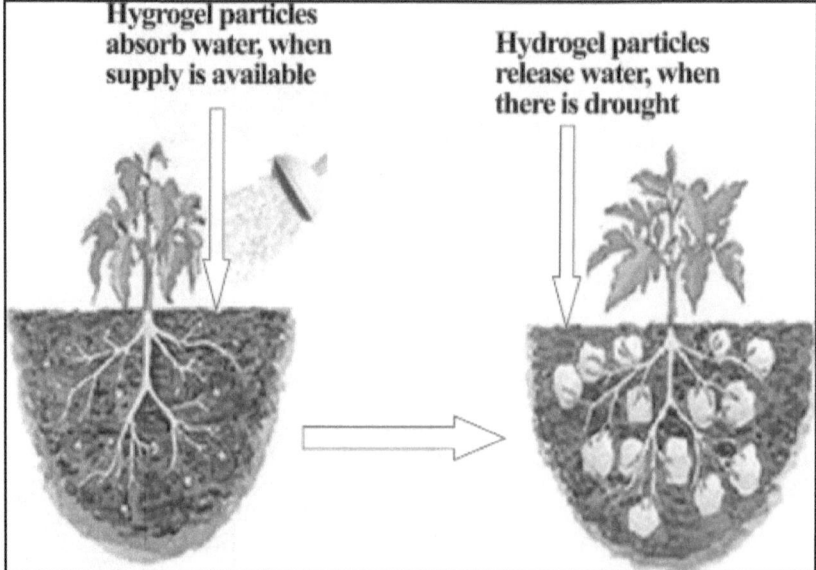

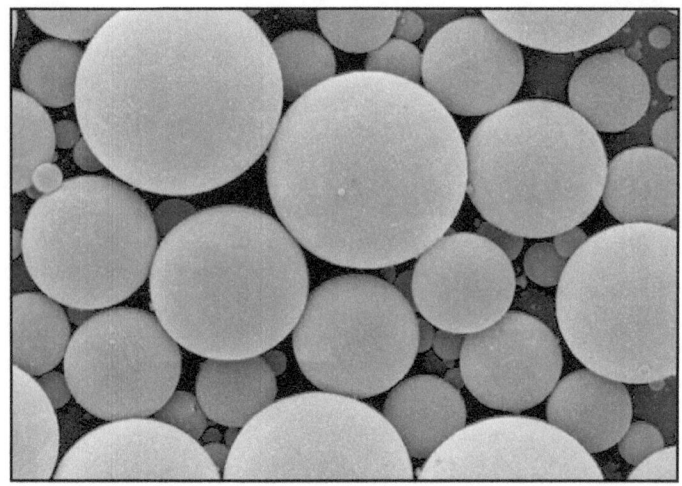

The key characteristics incorporated in AquaSoil® are:

1. Absorbance of water by 25 times its volume
2. Retention of water by 5 times more than the soil of the area of applications
3. Improvement of hydrological cycle
4. Generation of vermicular lives
5. Subsequently, the soil breaks down into silica particles.
6. These particles contain a lot of air voids in them, and so the soil becomes softer. Roots find it easier to blend into the soil.
7. Retards growth of grasses and weeds
8. Supplies nutrients to the soil

The novelties of the soil water retainers are more than one.

Novelty 01: AquaSoil® is aimed to be manufactured as a good water retainer because of its tiny particle size and large surface area with nooks and crannies available for water storage. Porosity in its particles allows the excess water to drain more readily and improves soil aeration. This property is likely to result in requirement of less water for crop growth.

Novelty 02: AquaSoil® has been tested as one of the best media for growing plants. It is possible to grow most plants in AquaSoil® alone, although usually the finer grades and medium grades will work better (R&D to be done) and require less water.

Novelty 03: AquaSoil® will prevent soil compaction (R&D to be done), improve aeration and retain moisture.

Novelty 04: AquaSoil® will also be used in propagation of new plants and seed cultivation, as well as in indoor container growing, composting, and on lawns.

Wealth from Waste

Nothing is a waste in this world. A stone for someone is gold for someone else. Ripe apples are a waste for the plant bearing it. Panicles are waste for the rice plant. But apple and rice are wealth (input materials) for humans. The stubble in agriculture land is a waste for the farmer but it is a fodder for cattle. Dung is a waste for the cow but cow dung is a fertilizer for crops. Tender coconut shells are a waste for the coconut vendor but the same is an input material for the coir manufacturer. So, there is nothing like 'waste'. Only hardship in the disposal process and the inability to find immediate use that make a material seem like a waste. But, in the real sense, every material is an input raw material for some process or the other.

So, in this section, we shall start discussing the 'thought process', which we may call 'design thinking', to describe the numerous materials which hitherto have been viewed as a 'waste'. Thus, the topic is better termed as 'conversion of one material to the another'. The entire gamut of cottage industries engaged in pottery, design and decoration of items from clay, coir and jute; skin cleansers from banana peels; bio fertilizers from food wastes; and agro wastes are a few examples in this area.

Nutraceuticals

Several nutraceuticals, food supplements and health products are available in the market. The market is flooded with products from companies like GlaxoSmithKline, Kellogg, Britannia and Dabur. We can find products such as energy drinks, full-grain biscuits, anti-diabetic biscuits, and *chyavanprash* on the shelves of grocery shops and supermarkets. There is no dearth of good products. On the other hand, there is a chunk of our population suffering from malnourishment and anaemia. Both these things are visible. This means that there is a gap. Supply and demand are not the issues. The gap is due to something else. The gap is because of the 'inability' to purchase the products listed above.

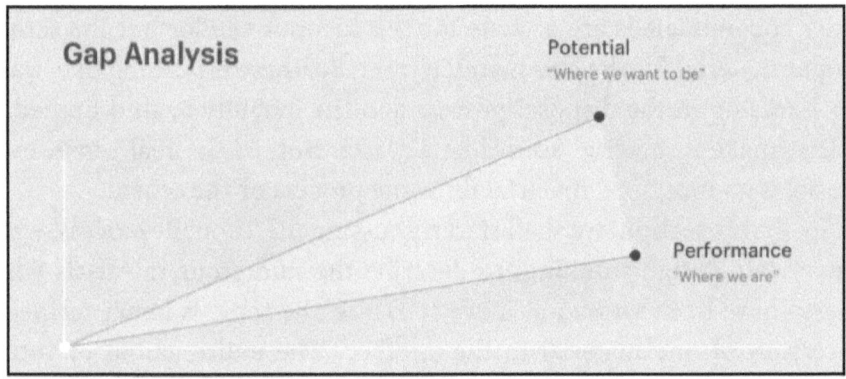

We shall deliberate on the points mentioned in the previous paragraph with special reference to the gap analysis between cost and quality. But, before that, we need to go a little further.

Certain data are painful to be presented even though the purpose of the said data is to bring out facts to the notice of the policy-makers of the nation. Our purpose is to make a serious effort to improve the current situation. We are talking about nutritional aspects with special reference to our country, to which we owe a lot.

As per the WHO's Global Nutrition Report (GNR), India has one-third of the world's stunted children. The GNR came into existence following the first Nutrition for Growth Initiative Summit (N4G) in 2013. The GNR was devised as a mechanism for tracking the commitments made by 100 stakeholders spanning governments, aid donors, civil society, the UN, and businesses. This report, in Indian profile, brought out the following facts.

1. About 46.6 million children in India suffer from stunting due to poor nutrition intake. India tops the list of countries followed by Nigeria (13.9 million) and Pakistan (10.7 million).

2. India is also the country with the highest number – i.e. 25.5 million – of children (out of the global total of 50.5 million children) who are 'wasted'. This is an even more severe indicator of acute malnutrition. This means about half of the stunted children are in India.

3. The household with the lowest incomes had the highest number of wasting (23.8 %) and stunting (50.7%) among children under the age of five years.

4. The nutrition status of children and adolescents aged between 5 and 19 years. 58.1 % of boys were underweight while 50.1 % girls were underweight.

5. More than half of all women of reproductive age (51.4%), whether or not they were pregnant, suffered from anaemia.

As citizens of India, it pains to read this fact sheet. But emotions and feelings are not going to give any solution. We need to bridge the gap between 'product' and 'cost'. If this bridge is constructed, then the above mentioned problems will not occur.

One of the authors, Manoj Kumar Patel, and his team have made a successful attempt in this regard and developed a new nutraceutical called EDINNOPOWDER. It is rich with nutrients, vitamins, dietary fibres, and minerals. The cost of this nutraceutical is less than that of products available in the market. Some basic information about this product: Photograph 01 shows the Edinnopowder prepared in laboratory scale. Photograph 02 shows one of the food nutrients made out of Edinnopowder.

Samples of laboratory-scale manufacture of the product Edinnopowder were analyzed. The results obtained have been given in the following table.

Sl. No.	Parameter	UoM	Edinnopowder
01	Energy	Kcal	342
02	Carbohydrate	g	76
03	Protein	g	6.4
04	Moisture	g	9.21
05	Fat	g	0.65
06	Ash	%	3.33
07	Minerals	g	1.35
08	Fibre	g	3.17
09	Calcium	mg	306
10	Fe	mg	5.14
11	Thiamin	mg	0.21
12	Niacin	mg	0.55

Edinnopowder is compatible with: (a) water, (b) aqueous solution of honey, (c) milk, (d) coconut milk, (d) tender coconut water, (e) aqueous solution of sugar and salt as an hydrating agent and energy drink, (f) neem powder, and many other food and food supplements. This is how design thinking can give rise to a solutions that citizenry can accept both with respect to cost and utility.

Government projects (GP)

GP 01: BIRAC

Biotechnology Industry Research Assistance Council (BIRAC) is set up by Department of Biotechnology (DBT), Government of India as an interface agency to strengthen and empower the emerging biotech enterprise to undertake strategic research and innovation, addressing nationally relevant product development needs.

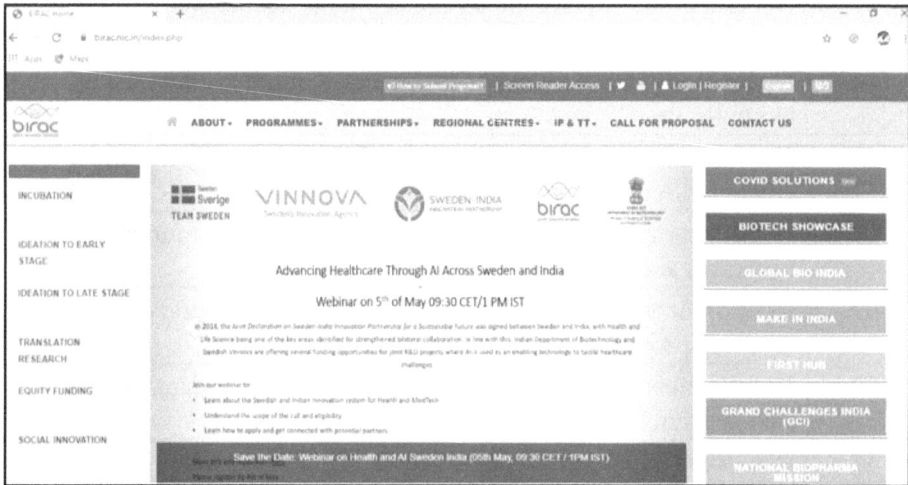

This is an industry-academia interface and implements its mandate through a wide range of impact initiatives—providing access to risk capital through targeted funding, technology transfer, IP management, and handholding schemes that help bring innovative excellence to biotech firms and make them globally competitive. In the last eight years, it has initiated several schemes, networks and platforms that have given affordable products through cutting-edge technologies.

These are some of the innovative ideas put forward by many design thinkers.

Sl. No	Title of the Project
01	A next-generation Coccidial solution
02	Development of dual-use microalgae for plant growth promotion and Orobanche weed control in agriculture
03	Waste = Food: Conversion of kitchen and agri-waste to organic nutrition to use in organic hydroponics
04	Development of recombinant single chain monoclonal antibodies to detect citrus greening pathogen caused by Candidatus Liberibacter asiaticus
05	Novel approach for secondary metabolite extraction vetiver oil and vetiver wax
06	Shelf life enhancement of perishable horticulture produce using biomolecules
07	Hyacinth Hunter: It is easy to remove hyacinth from water and convert into organic manure in low cost.
08	Development, optimisation and commercialization of functional beverages and value-added products made from tea
09	Development of novel indigenous probiotic with natural cholesterol-lowering properties
10	Development of a functional juice utilizing the abundant banana pseudo stem biomass
11	Duckweed based nutraceutical product
12	Naturally biodegradable personal hygiene products from rice/wheat straws to solve two major threats to environment
13	Preparation of activated carbon-based straw pen for drinking safe water during natural calamities
14	Innovation of a multi-purpose hybrid improved cook stove
15	A systematic approach to develop fortified edible cutlery
16	Upscaling and demonstration of pheromone application and mating dispenser technology for the management of codling moth to lift the ban on fresh fruits from Ladakh
17	PROBONE: Probiotic therapy to mitigate osteoporosis problem
18	Portable cold storages with proprietary thermal batteries to combat post-harvest losses
19	Formulation of ragi-based ready-to-serve food for paediatric nutrition
20	Bromelain production from pineapple wastes of NE India for food processing and medical applications

Sl. No	Title of the Project
21	Improvement in bone mineralization and development Vitamin D metabolites and iron enriched Whole milk substitute from transgenic goats
22	Development of EDINNOPOWDER: A nutrients rich agro product
23	Biological control of post-harvest diseases in perishable fruits and vegetables by bacillus bio surfactant lipopeptides
24	Automation in sericulture equipment
25	Production of bio based micro beads from agricultural residues
26	A cost effective, eco-friendly, biological degradation of raw chitin waste into chitosan and chitin oligosaccharides: a multifunctional bio products acts as bio-stimulant and crop protectants in agriculture
27	To demonstrate POC for operational biomass dryer which is cost effective, scalable 50 less operating cost as compare to available industrial dryers and quality of dehydrated fruits and vegetables matches the A-grade dried products
28	Economical clarification of sugarcane juice in jaggery and khandsari plant by electro coagulation technology
29	Cavitation based advanced technology for effective control of algae growth and in-situ degradation of organic pollutants
30	Natural air purifying system

GP 02: AGRI UDAAN

Agri Udaan is a food and agribusiness accelerator project for agritech start-ups organized by a-IDEA, Technology Business Incubator of NAARM, supported by the Department of Science and Technology. It is run by the Indian Council of Agricultural Research. This is basically a six-month programme where shortlisted agritech start-ups are guided in order to scale up stage innovators, entrepreneurs, and start-ups in the food and agribusiness sectors. The focussed areas of this project include smart agriculture, agri biotech, supply chain technology, animal husbandry, farm mechanisation, and farm-fresh retail.

GP 03: CROPIN

CropIn is a SaaS-based agritech start-up, which delivers future-ready farming solutions to the entire agricultural sector. Founded by Krishna

Kumar in 2010, the start-up utilizes cutting-edge technologies such as big data analytics, artificial intelligence, machine language and remote sensing to enable its clients to analyze and interpret data to derive real-time actionable insights on standing crops. In June 2018, the Department of Agriculture, Karnataka joined hands with this start-up to start a programme to helps farmers adopt smart farming techniques to increase the growth of their crops. Besides the Karnataka government, the start-up has also tied up with the Department of Horticulture in Andhra Pradesh in the districts of Krishna and Chittoor.

GP 04: MAHA AGRI TECH

The Maha Agri Tech project was launched in January 2019 for the welfare of farmers. It is one of South India's largest producers and marketers of bio products and seeds suppliers. It aims to empower Maharashtra farmers and modernize the field of agriculture. The project includes agritech bio products such as Maha Bullet, Maha Zyme, Maha Force, Maha M-Blast, Maha Shock, and Maha Bloom Plus. The Maha Agritech programme is also launched to solve agrarian problems with the help of satellites and drones.

GOVT SCHEMES (GS)

GS 01: PRIVATIZATION IN AGRI MARKET

On May 1, 2020, the Madhya Pradesh Chief Minister, Shri Shivraj Singh Chouhan, introduced a privatization plan for the first time in the history of Indian agriculture, especially for the benefit of farmers. According to this plan:

1. Private *mandis* will operate apart from the regular *mandis*.
2. Exporters, traders and food processors can open a private *mandi* and buy the agriculture produce by visiting the farmer's land or house.
3. Farmers in Madhya Pradesh can now sell their produce at more competitive prices, that too without going to the *mandis*.

4. The amendment in the *mandi* rules is aimed at giving freedom to the farmers to sell their produce at a better price and by their own choice.
5. There will be only one licence with which the private *mandis* can buy agricultural produce from all over the state, and the *mandi* fee will also be charged at only one place.
6. The state has also decided to launch an e-trading facility that will allow the state's farmers to trade with any other trading body across the country.
7. The government has kept the *mandi* tax unchanged; therefore, it is expected to keep the burden intact.
8. The fall in demand due to the lockdown (due to the Covid-19 pandemic) and the nearly banned exports will create an oversupply of agri produce with the farmers.

GS 02: eNAM

National Agriculture Market (eNAM) is a pan-India electronic trading portal, which networks the existing APMC (Agricultural Produce Market Committee) *mandis* to create a unified national market for agricultural commodities. Small Farmers Agribusiness Consortium is the lead agency for implementing eNAM under the aegis of Ministry of Agriculture and Farmers' Welfare, Government of India.

Its vision is to promote uniformity in agriculture marketing by streamlining procedures across the integrated markets, removing information asymmetry between buyers and sellers, and promoting real-time price discovery based on actual demand and supply.

The mission of the scheme is the integration of APMCs across the country through a common online market platform to facilitate pan-India trade in agricultural commodities, providing better price discovery through a transparent auction process based on the quality of produce along with timely online payment.

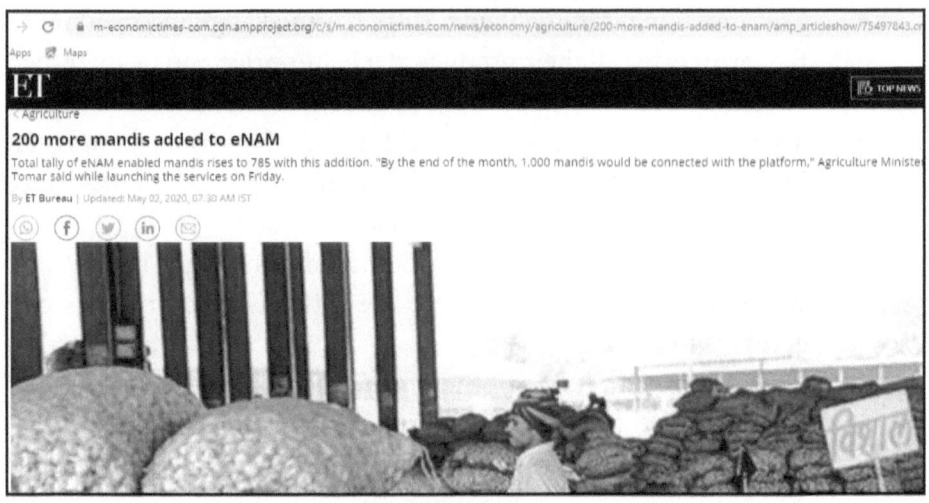

A piece of news emerged in the month of May (2020) when the manuscript of this book was getting finalized. The news said that the government had connected 200 new *mandis* across seven states to its national digital agricultural trading platform—eNAM—taking the total tally of eNAM-enabled *mandis* to 785. By the end of the month i.e. by 31st of May, about 1,000 *mandis* would be connected with the platform, said the Agriculture Minister, Narendra Singh Tomar, while launching the services.

Launched in April 2016, eNAM started with just 21 *mandis*. The number of registered farmers has risen to 1.66 crore, and 1.28 lakh traders transact on this platform.

More than 1,000 Farmer Producer Organisations (FPOs) have also been enrolled into this platform. So far, eNAM has registered a business of over Rs 1 lakh crore, helping farmers discover prices before selling their produce. Integration of eNAM with the Unified Market Platform of Karnataka's Rashtriya e-Market Services (ReMS), an e-trading platform promoted by the Karnataka State Agriculture Marketing Board, is being planned.

This is for the first time in India that two different e-trading platforms for agri commodities of this scale will be made interoperable. This will help farmers of Karnataka to sell their produce to a large number of traders registered with eNAM, and even farmers from eNAM *mandis* in other states will be able to sell their produce to Karnataka traders who are enrolled with the ReMS platform of Karnataka. This will also promote inter-state trade between the states on the eNAM platform and Karnataka.

GS 03: NMSA

The National Mission for Sustainable Agriculture (NMSA) has been formulated for enhancing agricultural productivity, especially in rainfed areas focussing on integrated farming, water use efficiency, soil health management, and synergizing resource conservation.

NMSA is designed to cater to the key dimensions of water use efficiency, nutrient management, and livelihood diversification through the adoption of a sustainable development pathway by progressively shifting to environmental friendly technologies, adoption of energy efficient equipment, conservation of natural resources, and integrated farming.

The schemes under NMSA are:

1. Rainfed Area Development (RAD): RAD is being implemented by RFS Division.
2. Soil Health Management (SHM): SHM is being implemented by INM Division.
3. Sub Mission on Agro Forestry (SMAF): SMAF is being implemented by NRM Division.
4. Paramparagat Krishi Vikas Yojana (PKVY): PKVY is being implemented by INM Division.
5. Soil and Land Use Survey of India (SLUSI): This is being implemented by RFS Division.
6. National Rainfed Area Authority (NRAA): This is being implemented by RFS Division.
7. Mission Organic Value Chain Development in North Eastern Region (MOVCDNER): This is being implemented by INM Division.
8. National Centre of Organic Farming (NCOF): This is being implemented by INM Division.
9. Central Fertilizer Quality Control and Training Institute (CFQC&TI): This is implemented by INM Division.

GS 04: PMKSY

The Pradhan Mantri Krishi Vikas Yojana or PMKSY has been formulated with the vision of extending the coverage of irrigation water to all agri lands (*har khet ko pani*) and improving water use efficiency (more crop per drop) in a focussed manner with an end-to-end solution for source creation, distribution, management, field application, and extension activities.

GS 05: PMVY

The Pradhan Mantri Krishi Vikas Yojana or PKVY, an initiative to promote organic farming in the country, was launched by the NDA government in 2015. According to the scheme, farmers are encouraged to form groups or clusters and take to organic farming methods over large areas in the country.

The aim is to form 10,000 clusters over the next three years and bring about 5 lakh acres of agricultural area under organic farming. The government also intends to cover the certification costs and promote organic farming through the use of traditional resources.

To avail themselves of the scheme, each cluster or group must have 50 farmers willing to take up organic farming under PKVY and possess a total area of at least 50 acres. Each farmer enrolling in the scheme will be provided INR 20,000 per acre by the government, spread over three years.

GS 06: PMFVY

The Pradhan Mantri Fasal Bima Yojana or PMFBY is a government-sponsored crop insurance scheme that integrates multiple stakeholders onto a single platform.

It has been implemented to fulfil the following objectives:

1. To provide insurance coverage and financial support to farmers in the event of failure of any of the notified crop as a result of natural calamities, pests and diseases
2. To stabilize the income of farmers to ensure their continuance in farming

3. To encourage farmers to adopt innovative and modern agricultural practices
4. To ensure flow of credit to the agriculture sector

GS 07: GRAMIN BHANDARAN YOJANA

In regards to storage of produces, the Gramin Bhandaran Yojana has been started with many objectives.

1. To create scientific storage capacity with allied facilities in rural areas
2. To meet the requirements of farmers for storing farm produce, processed farm produce, and agricultural inputs
3. To promote grading, standardization, and quality control of agricultural produce to improve their marketability
4. To prevent distress sale immediately after harvest by providing the facility of pledge financing and marketing credit by strengthening agricultural marketing infrastructure in the country

GS 08: MIF

Through the Micro Irrigation Fund or MIF, the government has approved a dedicated Rs 5,000-crore fund to bring more land area under micro irrigation as part of its objective to boost agricultural production and farmers' income.

The fund has been set up under NABARD, which will provide this amount to states at a concessional rate of interest to promote micro irrigation, which currently has a coverage of only 10 million hectares as against the potential of 70 million hectares.

Other Promising Results of Design Thinking

Agriculture is the backbone of India. Post-independence, however, this sector did not receive attention like industry and industrial development. There were many projects made available to farmers and the agricultural sectors.

But the government in India, with effect from the year 2014, has gifted many innovative schemes. These schemes are the result of analysis and design thinking. Most of these are practical and useful. The following are a few among them:

1. high yield crops and agri produce
2. biofertilizers
3. disease preventing spices
4. earthworm generating composts
5. from food leftovers
6. water conservation
7. Jal Shakti Aviyan
8. crops requiring less water
9. soil nutrients
10. soil health card

Conclusion

A large number of innovative products, processes and schemes have come up in the recent past through design thinking or out-of-the-box thinking. We have described some of these products, processes and schemes in some depth in the previous sections of this chapter. There are many more innovative ideas and concepts that facilitate quantity and quality outputs in many areas of agriculture. The purpose of this chapter is to generate a curiosity in the mind of the reader to delve further into design thinking in agriculture. We also encourage continued reading on the subject by surfing literature in good websites, which are in plenty. In the reference section, we have tried to list out some of the good sources of literature in this direction.

05

Design Thinking in Entrepreneurship

Introduction

Recently, design thinking was introduced to students in non-design related disciplines such as business and management as a tool for decision-making in other fields. When it comes to design thinking in design schools, it is focussed on thinking beyond the output of the product, on modelling the work, system or service, and design students are expected to apply their design thinking abilities to non-design related problems. Design thinking finds a special place in different departments of many schools such as Stanford D. School, HPI, MIT, University of Virginia, and London Business School. It has also flourished in these schools.

The rise of the culture of entrepreneurship in start-ups begins with the differences between small-scale and big companies. Start-ups are not the smaller version of big companies. Thus, ideas applied to big companies cannot be applied to start-ups. The small companies and start-ups differ from big companies with respect to their flexibility levels and contexts. In general parlance, a start-up is set up by an entrepreneur who takes risks in new ideas and products. The entrepreneur develops new products, processes and services by making 'mistakes'. The process of bringing out new products, processes and services through mistake proofing is the basis of design thinking. Practice-based knowledge is worthier than planning and thinking, and it can only be made possible by the entrepreneur. Newness and new product development are very important.

The growth of a nation depends on national policies, which control and accelerate the economy, culture as well as the overall development of the country. Proper management of human resources plays a major role in the smooth functioning of the nation. Entrepreneurs are the important entities who support the national economy as well as employment generation, converting sustainable resources into products for a stronger economy.

If we analyze the movement from an agricultural economy to industrial development, and then to revolution of technology, software and analytics, we are moving faster to achieve a stronger economy by involving entrepreneurs in exploring natural resources, deployment of geospatial technology, block chain technology, environment-friendly skills and performance, strong MIS using huge numbers of authentic databases, real-time decision-making, implementation of powerful apps, data networking, ERPs, and design thinking. Design thinking is being continuously applied for better economic development. The new generations of entrepreneurs (start-ups) are encouraged to play a major role in employment generation as well as a stronger economy for a dedicated political leadership.

A study carried out by Ozan Soyupak and Humanur Bagli on entrepreneurship and design thinking concluded important findings. The study was significant in terms of investigating how design thinking affects the start-up culture as a catalyst, in which phase of the projects design thinking is more relevant and effective, how design thinking reveals missing and premature aspects of entrepreneurship projects, and how it can be held as a promising tool for design education. The study links business and entrepreneurship literature with design education. According to the gathered data, the contributions of the long-termed collaboration between industrial design education and the start-up ecosystem to the start-ups can be summed up in the following manner: developing user-centred research and data collection, gaining awareness, developing user-cantered perspective, and design consultancy.

Entrepreneurs

Entrepreneurs are the backbone of the development process. In simple terms, an entrepreneur is a person who takes the risk of converting new ideas into reality. He or she is the person who habitually creates and innovates something to build recognized value through perceived opportunities.

Entrepreneurship is the purposeful activity of an individual or a group of associated individuals undertaking to initiate, maintain or aggrandize profit by production or distribution of economic goods and services. It is relevant to mention here that an entrepreneur is innovative, creative, risk-taking, and organized. The qualities he necessarily possesses are common sense, specialized knowledge in the field, self-confidence, ability to get things done, creativity, leadership, communication, willingness to take risk, self-motivation and determination.

1. Complex problem solving

- Complexity is defined as the number of variables or inputs in a system. Take managing a team as an example. Each additional team member adds their own desires, competencies, work patterns, and perspectives to the team.
- This makes the team more complex—because of the new members' inputs and also the interactions of their inputs with the existing inputs of the team.
- Basically, every new factor makes a problem exponentially more complex. Skilled people can grapple with this complexity and derive strategies and outputs from them.

2. Critical thinking

Critical thinking goes hand in hand with complex problem solving. The simple definition of critical thinking is clear and logical argument construction done through clear definitions of statements and then organizing them into arguments or conclusions.

3. Creativity

The Innovators DNA defines creativity as:

- Your ability to generate innovative ideas is not merely a function of the mind but also a function of five key behaviour that optimize your brain for discovery.

- These five key behaviour are:

  i. **Associating:** Drawing connections between questions, problems or ideas from unrelated fields
  ii. **Questioning:** Posing queries that challenge common wisdom
  iii. **Observing:** Scrutinizing the behaviour of customers, suppliers and competitors to identify new ways of doing things
  iv. **Networking:** Meeting people with different ideas and perspectives
  v. **Experimenting:** Constructing interactive experiences and provoking unorthodox responses to see what insights emerge

- This model is fascinating for a number of reasons.

  i. It shows the leaps humans uniquely make, once we (i) understand the problem and (ii) find the patterns, thus enabling us to (iii) synthesize solutions.
  ii. Each of these individual activities can be done by anyone, and creativity is then being done in aggregate, which means creativity can be trained.

4. People management

There are two components of people management.

  i. **People:** This means EQ, inspiring, motivating, encouraging and leading.
  ii. **Management:** This means hiring, firing, training, disciplining, evaluating and directing.

These two components may seem at odds with each other. But effective managers expertly balance both as they move their team towards their goal. This may be as a representative of a corporation attempting to meet some strategic goal. The main job of the people manager is to draw out the best from the people around them. Top-to-bottom organizational leaders enable success.

5. Coordinating with others

- People management inherently has power imbalances between the manager and the employee or the team leader and the team member. The most powerful entrepreneurs know how to operate when they are on either side of the equation and when they are balanced with their peer.
- This peer could be a fellow manager, an entrepreneur, an investor, a partner, or a stakeholder in your field. The point here isn't looking out at the world and seeing a hierarchy.
- It's about recognizing when there are mutual dependencies and when those dependencies are one-sided or situation-specific. For example, employees rely on employers for income, while employers rely on employees for output. Whereas fellow entrepreneurs may rely on each other for mutual benefits to their business model.

6. Emotional intelligence

- Emotional intelligence is being able to understand and manage the emotions of yourself and others. It includes three skills.
- Emotional awareness — knowing when and what feelings are present in ourselves and others. It includes emotional literacy, which is the ability to label the emotions and act upon them. At its highest level, one can anticipate emotions from external and internal stimuli and thus regulate them over time.
- Harnessing emotions — after awareness and literacy, or recognizing and understanding, comes acting on the emotions to enable healthy relationships with others, and with ourselves. Once we control our emotions, we can lead interactions with others, diffuse tense situations, and generally lead those around us in a mutually beneficial way.

- Managing emotions — the culmination of the previous two skills in being able to anticipate, understand, harness and then manage emotions proactively. Instead of reacting, we respond with the appropriate emotion. Need calmness to focus on some task? The emotionally intelligent manager can regulate their internal state to create that emotional presence. The same applies for creating enthusiasm for a task in a team.

7. Judgement and decision-making

- Judgement and decision-making is a combination of complex problem solving, critical thinking, creativity, people management, coordination and emotional intelligence.
- It's being able to analytically assess a situation, understand the implications, recognize the scope and possibilities, harness organizational resources, both internally and externally, and oversee the implementation of solutions.
- This is an extremely hard thing to do consistently, and it requires great mental discipline, willpower and focus. The most effective entrepreneurs do this daily. They escape the trap of putting out the day's fires, and instead focus on solving the organization's highest level problems. The ones you, as a leader, can't see today; the problems firms are running towards without realizing them.

8. Service orientation

- Service orientation is defined as:

The ability and desire to anticipate, recognize and meet others' needs, sometimes even before those needs are articulated.

9. Negotiation

- Negotiation is the process by which parties mediate differences. Ideally, compromises or agreements are reached, which avoid arguments and disputes. The principles driving negotiation are:
  a. Fairness
  b. Mutual benefit
  c. Maintaining relationships

- To effectively negotiate, a leader needs a clear understanding of their current position, as well as their desired outcome; the path connecting these two creates their strategy.

10. Cognitive flexibility

- Cognitive flexibility has two components.
  - The ability to switch between thinking about two different concepts
  - The ability to think about multiple concepts simultaneously

- Cognitive flexibility draws on one's critical thinking (what is and isn't) and one's creativity (what could be).
- As an entrepreneur, you're constantly switching between different tasks, and dealing with different variations of similar problems. The more you reduce your cognitive 'switching cost' and the better you synthesize new solutions from varying fields and disciplines, the better equipped you are to operate in an environment of uncertainty and speed. This is what most entrepreneurs do.

Entrepreneurship

Entrepreneurship is an applied discipline. It is more often than not taught and researched as if it is a natural science. Entrepreneurs think and, to some extent, act like designers, highlighting alignment in divergent and convergent ways around identifying and then acting on realizing what could be in response to an opportunity or a problem.

This requires skills in observation, synthesis, searching and generating alternatives, critical thinking, feedback, visual representation, creativity, problem solving, and value creation. This is quite a range and depth of skills for educators to enable and facilitate.

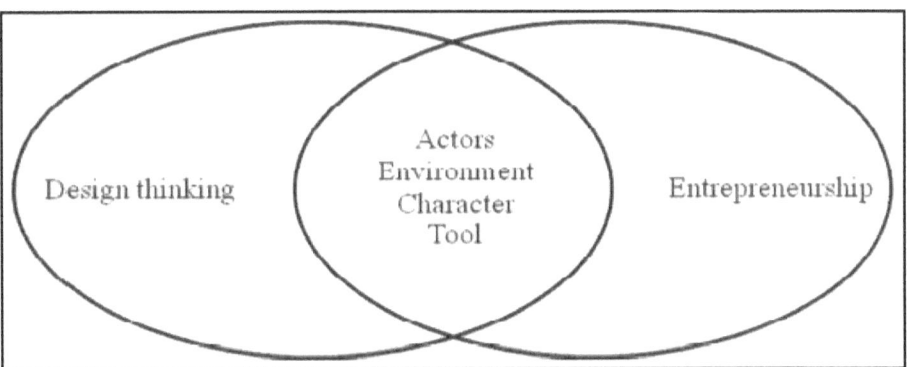

Design thinking is fundamentally concerned with human needs. Proponents of design thinking such as Tim Brown, Chief Executive Officer of IDEO, highlight that it is not a "linear, milestone-based process". Rather, it is an interaction between three spaces: *inspiration, ideation and implementation.* Brown argues that design tools can be effectively utilized in other disciplines, such as business and education, to overcome the 'we know the solution' approach.

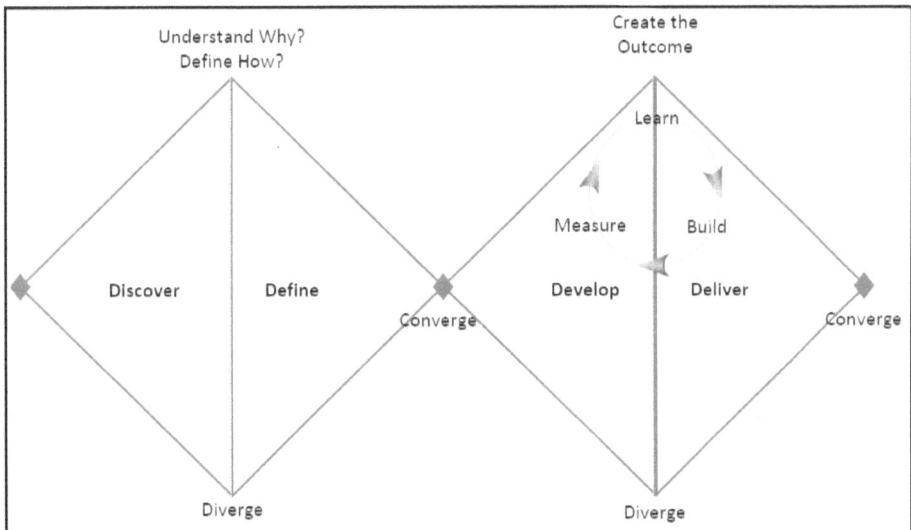

This design thinking approach to course design and development in an entrepreneurship programme was first trialled in 2007. The design and development concepts utilized the Double Diamond Model that addresses four key iterative cycles in the design process: *Discover, Define, Develop,*

Deliver. This model also underpinned the later development of a social entrepreneurship course in which problem-based learning was matched to design thinking tools such as rapid prototyping, proof of concept via codesign, service-blueprinting, and role-play to enhance students' capacity to think analytically, intuitively and divergently.

Entrepreneurship Development

Entrepreneurship development is essentially an educational process and an endeavour in human resource development. It is an environment in which an entrepreneur can learn and discharge functions. It is designed with the aim of encouraging self-employment. It imparts training and motivates existing and potential entrepreneurs to start a new business, diversify or expand the existing business. It helps in employment and wealth creation among the educated unemployed youth. It makes them well-equipped to face risks and challenges as entrepreneurs. The government needs considerable human and material resources in this regard, as these are important to detailed planning and implementation.

Objectives of entrepreneurship development

- Accelerating industrial development by enlarging pool of entrepreneurs
- Assessing industrial development of rural and less developed areas
- Enlarging small and medium enterprise sector
- Providing productive self-employment
- Improving performance of small industries
- Diversifying sources of entrepreneurship, thereby promoting dispersal of business

Stages of entrepreneurship development

- Basic training or pre-training
- Training or development
- Post-training or follow-up

Limitations of entrepreneurship development

- Developing all-round, competent and successful first-generation entrepreneurs
- Generating viable opportunities for permanent self-employment

Lessons from entrepreneurship development

- Comprehensive as against a partial approach
- Integrated approach
- Development approach
- Goal-oriented concerns
- Need-based flexibility
- Individual counselling
- Introspective critical attitude

Focus Areas for An Entrepreneur

If someone feels that their life has meaning, they're more likely to become an entrepreneur. And it goes even deeper than that. There is a pattern in the people who are entrepreneurs. They are most energized, confident, and goal-focussed, and they believe that they can live meaningful lives. Regardless of whether or not they have plans to start a business, respondents surveyed believed strongly in their ability to live meaningful lives. They also had the most positive views about entrepreneurs. In short, meaning in life inspires the entrepreneurial spirit as well as the public opinions needed to make our society supportive of entrepreneurship.

When we say 'meaning in life', we mean the feeling that you play a significant role in the world. It's a sense of having a purpose. To feel meaningful is to believe that one matters, that one can make important contributions to the family, friends, communities, and the broader society.

It has powerful implications for physical and mental wellbeing, confidence, motivation, and optimism about the future. Decades of research in psychology has shown the importance of this feeling in making people resilient and focussed during difficult times. And here's why it is very important to understand this now: If we can take advantage of the power of meaning, then aspiring entrepreneurs can rise and provide the resilience and focus necessary to help us all navigate these difficult times.

Entrepreneurs can harness this power. No matter where they are in their entrepreneurial journey, they start by taking the time to focus on what currently gives their life meaning. Then, they think about how their entrepreneurial ambitions build on that. For most of them, the 'meaning' is found in close relationships—by connecting with and serving the ones they love. This is helpful when developing a business plan—to think about how the plan will not only help one pursue their ambitions but also benefit those they care about the most. For example, in building a business, one can plan possibilities that can provide opportunities for family and friends. Entrepreneurs may also consider whether the plan would give them the ability to spend more time with loved ones, or whether it would offer new ways for them to be present for their loved ones.

More broadly, 'meaning in life' helps entrepreneurs think about how one's future business can help make significant contributions to one's community, and perhaps even the broader world. Focussing on the meaningful role that one can play not only helps inspire oneself, but also helps one to generate novel ideas and innovative solutions. Entrepreneurs may be the ones who help make important breakthroughs, the ones who find a way to help vulnerable populations in the community, or the ones who find a new way to deliver goods and services to meet people's needs during physical distancing.

Eventually, when the global challenges pass, economic recovery will depend on entrepreneurial spirit and business innovations to help our society flourish. As people continue, at least in the short term, to reduce their travel, limit their retail shopping and dining out, avoid attending large events and meetings, and continue other social distancing behaviour, businesses will need to explore new ways of producing and delivering goods and services. New opportunities will arise for those who can innovate in this environment. Also, individuals will need to support entrepreneurs and their businesses for them to rebuild themselves and thrive.

Entrepreneurship in rural India

Agriculture in India continues to be the backbone of rural society. It accounts for about 70 per cent of the total workforce of the country. Again, continuous growth of population led to overcrowding on agricultural land, diminishing farm produce, and migration of farm workers in large numbers to the urban areas.

Entrepreneurship could take off the excess labour from the farms, which causes disguised employment. Rural entrepreneurship can simply be defined as entrepreneurship emerging in the rural areas. In other words, establishing industrial units in the rural areas refers to rural entrepreneurship.

Rural entrepreneurship is, in essence, entrepreneurship that ensures value addition to rural resources in rural areas, engaging largely with rural human resources. This means that finished products are produced in rural areas out of the resources obtained in rural areas by largely rural people.

Types of rural industries

- **Agro-based industries:** sugar, jaggery, oil processing from oil seeds, pickles, fruit juice, spices, dairy products, etc
- **Forest-based industries:** wood products, bamboo products, honey, coir industry, plates from leaves, etc
- **Mineral-based industry:** stone crushing, cement, red oxide, wall coating powder, etc
- **Textile industry:** spinning, weaving, colouring, bleaching, etc
- **Engineering and services:** agriculture equipment, tractors, pump sets repairs, etc

Software applications in entrepreneurship

Design thinking is used by Apple, Google, Samsung and GE by placing the **user at the centre.** The core concept behind these companies is to be open to users and their actual needs and concerns.

Books about novel design methods and how to use them in practice were published as early as 1940. Rudolf Arnheim wrote a book about visual thinking in 1969 (*Visual Thinking*), **which is still one of the key publications on artistic thinking and education.** In parallel, major universities such as Stanford and MIT started to research the main features of the ways of thinking of successful designers in various fields and **how their thinking could be applied in other areas.** Peter Rowe's book titled

Design Thinking was published in 1987 and it describes the role of the design thinking method in urban planning and architecture. Nowadays, the most recognized proponent of the method is Tim Brown, CEO of the innovation and design firm IDEO, located in Silicon Valley, who regularly publishes articles on the topic.

Geospatial technology in entrepreneurship

Geospatial technology is a valuable support system for retail business. Retail companies are under pressure today with modern-day shoppers being more demanding than ever. Retailers have to constantly rethink their marketing strategies and react in real-time to competition and customers with a mobile phone in hand. GIS (geographic information systems), frequently referred to as location intelligence or geospatial technology (GT), is a powerful big data technique that combines seemingly unrelated data to create powerful insights that would not have been apparent in a spreadsheet. GT works by mixing location-based information (customer address, sales territories and delivery routes) with business information like sales figures, product inventory and delivery routes, thus enabling retailers to do everything from customer profiling and site selection to supply chain optimization and competitor analysis. There are three ways in which retail companies can employ location intelligence to boost their bottom line—in order to solve complex business problems and improve operational decision-making.

GIS technology helps the retailer in:

a. measuring and visualizing market trends,
b. profiling customers, and
c. selecting the right sites.

Software in Entrepreneurship

A large majority of computer systems are dependent on a storage system. Knowledge on databases is accumulated over time. But, along the way, somewhere here or there, designs mistakes may have crept in, causing data loss and outages. In data heavy systems, databases are the core of system design goals and trade-offs.

Over the last couple of years, there has been a growing interest in organizations to go 'agile'—that is finding efficient methods to iterate and deliver services and products quickly and efficiently. These agile technologies play a vital role in a competitive environment. The desire to move swiftly and efficiently is not specific to the area of software development alone; hence, naturally, agile has found its way to other areas too, such as design and marketing where there is a need to address aggressive deadlines and complex delivery.

Some important points on service design going agile are:

a. rethinking on deliverables and being leaner,
b. evolving the design thinking process to have fewer waterfalls,
c. creating a working group of makers, and
d. integrating the role of the product.

User payer system

When it comes to creating a platform ecosystem for different user payments, there is no end to the scenarios for user journeys. Yet, in order to bring continuous value to platform users, the best ways to design a mutual interaction based on the possible network effects are based on three different stages: (a) increasing users' engagement from content, (b) supporting more content creation financially and socially, and (c) creating a flywheel from a combination of (a) and (b).

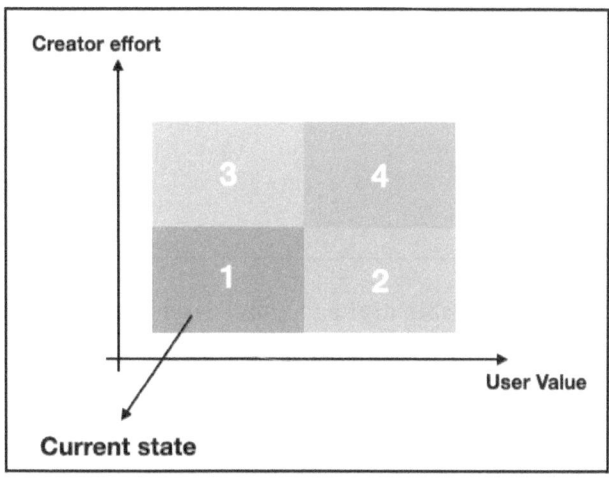

Platform designing

Platforms have become an indispensable part of our lives, and it is human nature to try to take control of everything going on there. Yet, when it comes to user controls, contrary to popular opinion, they are not more the merrier. The purpose of having user controls is to make users feel 'in control'.

Users really feel in control when user controls allow them to:

a. know something new,
b. choose their settings intentionally,
c. revert their settings, and
d. access user controls easily and intuitively.

All of these can be categorized into three dimensions: informative, understandable and accessible.

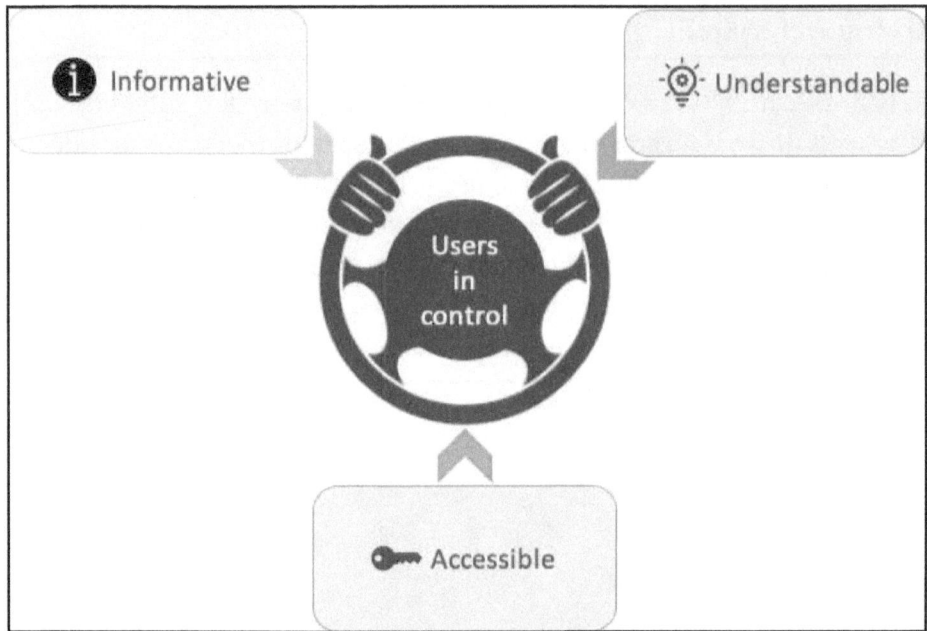

(Informative, understandable and accessible user controls make users feel in control.)

Informative

Platform developers use the same practice that they have learnt from privacy. Overwhelming users with a laundry list of settings all at once is not going to work. Users are more than likely to dismiss or make bad decisions. Platforms should prioritize useful and relevant settings to users. They should also explain why they want to give the users these controls and how these controls can improve their experiences on their platforms. Showing them their good intentions also helps gain users' trust of the platforms.

Understandable

Understandability is beyond the understanding of the text itself. Users should understand why they may need user controls, what these controls are for, how these controls work, and how they help make decisions. Providing guidance can help users to understand the settings and make the right decision that improves their user experience.

Accessible

Users should be able to find the user controls easily and intuitively whenever they want to change their controls. Low and high tech literate users have different perceptions and needs for user controls.

High tech literate users may confidently express how they would control their mobile app or social networking profiles, while medium to low tech literate users may struggle with understanding what the controls are for.

As low tech literate users represent a significant group of social networking platforms, it would be crucial for platform developers to include them when they evaluate whether the user controls are informative, understandable and accessible. Designing for low tech literate users is designing for everyone.

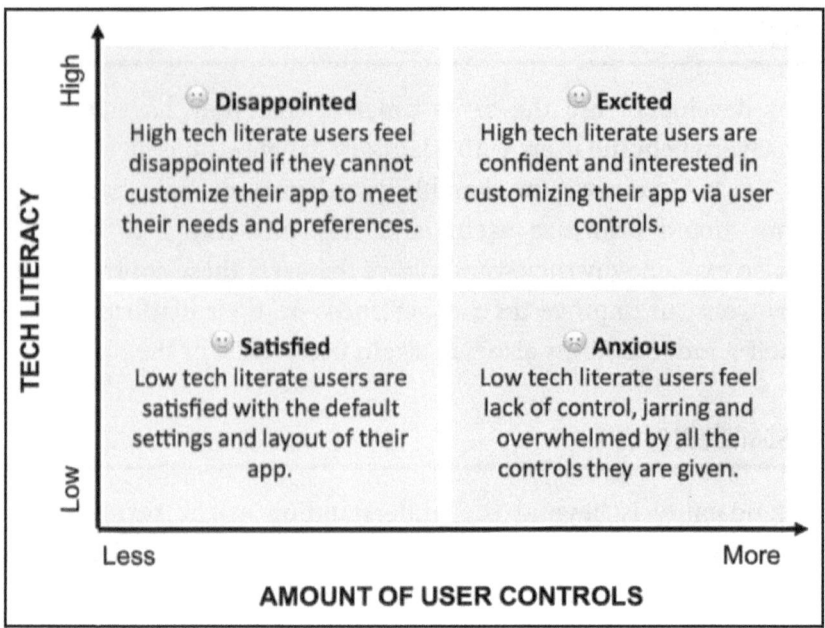

Informativeness and understandability

When the user controls show up, high tech literate users may confidently interact with the user controls and propose what else they want to customize. In contrast, low tech literate users may be anxious and confused. While user controls are informative and understandable to high tech literate users, they are not so to low tech literate users.

Accessibility

In terms of accessibility, the recommendation is to include both hidden gestures and visual elements to access user controls to accommodate different tech literacy and mental models based on research studies.

Technology-based ventures

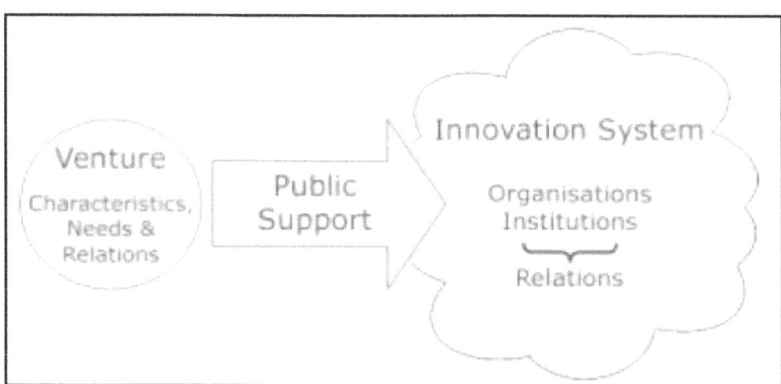

Practical examples of ways in which public actors can facilitate the linking process could be through measures such as finance—to develop or protect a product, investigate or work up the market, and develop the business concept. Advice about how to decide in critical situations, education, coaching and training to improve competencies are other ways in which this can be done. Support is about measures that increase factors such as investment readiness, motivation, the driving forces of the entrepreneur, and the credibility of the entrepreneur(s)/venture(s). All these factors make the venture 'more attractive' in the eyes of external factors such as customers, investors, suppliers, partners and presumptive employees, hence enabling the linking process of the venture.

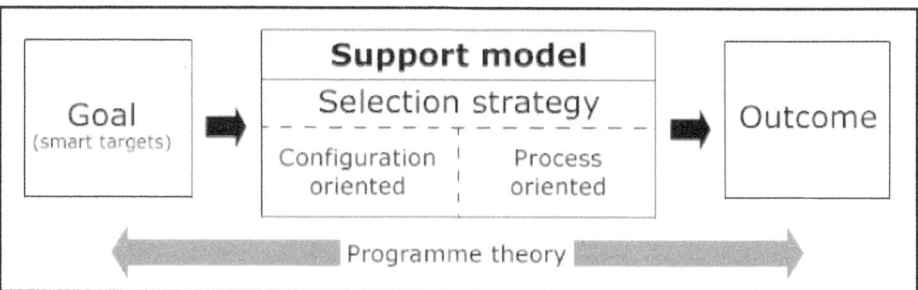

(The parts and components of a public entrepreneurship support programme.)

The practical implications regarding public support to trust but verify could be summarized in the following manner:

a. To help the ventures link to the information system, the support must enable the ventures in the entire early development process, not just parts or aspects thereof.

b. The support needs to be conformed to the groups that are targeted by the intervention. In addition, a consistent programme theory and evaluative awareness are needed.

c. Long-term commitment, information about present initiatives, and cooperation among support actors are needed.

Confrontation Programme Theory

Trying to capture scope that is too broad, instead on focussing on specific target groups and their needs, may jeopardize the programme logic and, thereby, the outcome as well. For example, an independent inventor who starts a firm in order to generate self-employment or to commercialize a patent for an uncomplicated product has needs that are quite different from the needs of a corporate spinoff venture or a research based start-up venture with a complex product that requires years of research. Hence, instead of trying to create 'one-stop-shops', it seems that diversification and specialization are the better ways to opt.

Furthermore, it is shown that it is difficult to evaluate new and especially innovative technologies at an early stage, because of the limited information that is available. Therefore, it is recommended that support to ventures in the earliest stages of development should be given in the form of a combination of advice and smaller subsidies or loans to a broader target group. Then, when the ventures have developed further, more rigorous selections can be undertaken, both by private and public actors. If public support works in this way, it increases its likelihood of acting as a complement to the market.

With regard to evaluation, it is highly important that policy-makers ensure that their programmes have developed an evaluative awareness. This implies that evaluation has to be a part of the programmes, from the very beginning. This enables learning and also allows specific data to be collected from the evaluation of strategic programmes.

Application specific

Entrepreneurship is one area that is replete with examples of design thinking. One of the authors has an industry experience of about four decades. Thus, practical examples can be drawn up here for the benefit of the reader.

Walk in the shoes of your customer/user

Before globalization, i.e. before 1991, India had only three high-energy manufacturing facilities. The number has now grown to about 50. The most interesting part is that the earlier three manufacturers have now been pulled down to lower positions due to various issues including their inability to empathize with the users. The users here are mines and mineral industries. The profits of the older companies too have become thin. On the other hand, the companies those came into existence after 1991 have prospered. In fact, one of the hitherto dealers has now become the best manufacturer of high-energy materials. These companies are the game changers. They have done a few unique things.

They are:

i.   They empathized with the users.

ii.   They put themselves in the shoes of the customer.

iii.   They developed good R&D and started producing prototypes for quick assessment.

iv.   They created acceptability of the prototypes by walking together with the users.

v.   They converted the prototypes into products for commercialization. This means the pace of each stride (conceptualization → laboratory trials → prototype → trials in the market → feedback collection → production scale-up) was fast.

vi.   They understood that users prefer both quality and cost. They realized that the illogic of standalone strength of either quality or cost was business suicide.

vii.   The successful companies embraced design thinking as their business mantra.

Conclusion

Entrepreneurs gain awareness of design and design thinking concepts after a user-centred perspective is developed. By completing the five stages of design thinking, entrepreneurs run user-centred researches independently and collect related data. In addition to the contributions to the start-ups, this also serves in the development of technical abilities and management skills among participating industrial design students.

The governments of different countries have taken initiatives to establish a synthetic relation between design and start-ups through a design education initiative. The Central Board of Secondary Education in India has taken a very appropriate step by introducing design thinking as a subject in the curriculum of schools. This will help students to think differently and innovatively. It will also give scope to students to ideate on different subjects instead of engaging in the conventional thinking process.

To conclude, the placement of design thinking in the entrepreneurship ecosystem and the placement of entrepreneurship in design education and other possible collaborations is worthwhile in terms of development for every stakeholder.

Case Studies

1. Packing Boxes

Packing boxes are required for all types of products. The company ABCD produces energy materials and high-energy materials. Energy materials and high-energy materials have different characteristics and it is important to know about these properties.

Energy materials have the following properties:

a.   They are fluid in nature.
b.   They are water-resistant, shockproof, fireproof, and impact-proof materials.
c.   The primary packing is done using polythene materials, and they are packed like milk sachets.
d.   Boxes should be completely overlapping.
e.   The weight of each box should be less than or equal to 25 kg.
f.   Boxes need to be piled up to five stacks.

High-energy materials have the following characteristics:

a.   They are solid in nature, and their shapes do not change when one piece is placed over many others.
b.   These are highly sensitive to shock, friction, fire, and electric discharges and drops.
c.   The weight of each box should not exceed 10 kg.
d.   The boxes can be stacked up to five stacks only.

Due to their differences in safety characteristics, shapes and forms (fluid in one case and solid in another case), the packing boxes were designed and in vogue since the 1960s. Energy materials were required to be packed in cardboard boxes having an overlapping design. High-energy materials, on the other hand, were packed in wooden boxes. These photographs show how these two types of boxes looked earlier.

The primary objective of doing business is to earn a profit in an ethical manner. So, the costs of the input materials play an important role in the internal business processes of the organization. In these particular cases, the costs of boxes were increasing. On the other hand, packing boxes were a non-functional input material in energy materials—in the sense the boxes did not take part in enhancing the performance of the packed products, in any manner. So, the need was to reduce the costs of the packing boxes. The efforts of the quality control department commenced with the reduction in the number of plies in the boxes (for cardboard boxes) and reduction in the quality of wood (for wooden boxes). But the customers down the line voiced their dissatisfaction over these changes. So, the manufacturers of the energy materials had to go back to the original packing that they had been using for decades. Therefore, thinking or 'normal thinking' did not yield financial advantages to the manufacturers. Now you see how a change in thinking made the process acceptable to all in the value chain.

In the case of the cardboard boxes, the changes suggested and the logic placed before the statute enforcing authorities and customers are:

| Sl. No. | Parameter | Changes | | Advantages | | | |
		From	To	Statute	Customer	Environment	Manufacturer
1	Number of plies	7 plies	5 plies	Laid down standards were met	Not affected	Natural resources are saved	Cost reduction
2	Weight of empty box	1 kg	0.8 kg				
3	Compression load	7 stacks	10 stacks			Unchanged	
4	Overlapping of flaps	Complete	Partial			Natural resource are saved	
5	Number of stitching clips	16	8				
6	Polythene lamination	Present	Removed				
7	Stack test	24 hours	48 hours			Unchanged	

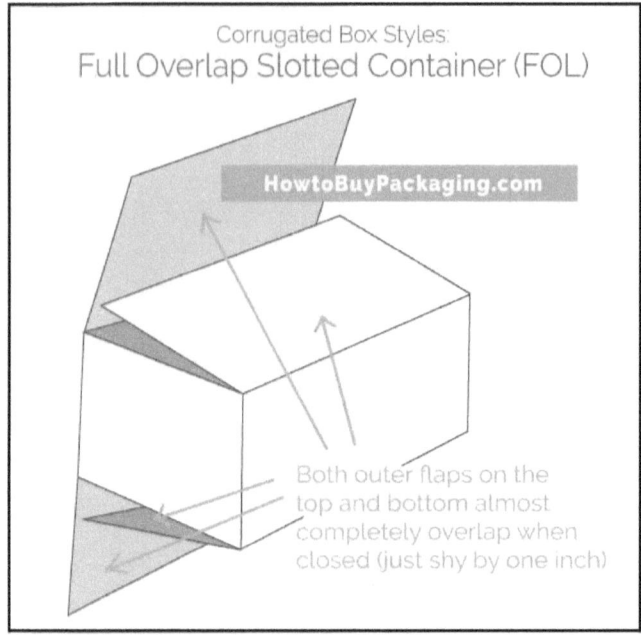

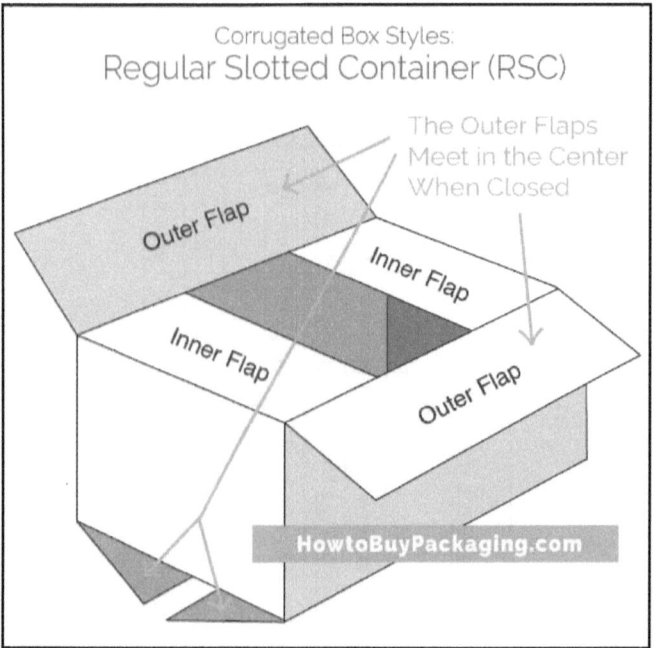

In the case of the wooden boxes, changes in both material and design were made. These changes were acceptable to all.

Sl. No.	Parameter	Changes		Advantages			
		From	To	Statute	Customer	Environment	Manufacturer
1	Wood type	Pine	Mango	Laid down standards were met	Not affected	Natural resources are saved	Cost reduction
2	Weight of empty box	12	7				
3	Compression load	7 stacks	7 stacks				

A packing specialist has now suggested trying out plywood in the place of mango wood.

This will work out to be advantageous from the following points of view:

i.   environment (trees will not be cut for packing such materials)
ii.   ease of availability
iii.   light weight (this will benefit the workers who handle the packaging)
iv.   reduction in costs

Thus, we find that problems and bottlenecks are overcome by thinking differently. The process is subsumed into the scope of design thinking because the thought itself was designed and the designed thought is thus transformed into a product.

2. Green Fireworks

For those not conversant with the term 'Deepavali', it is to be mentioned that it is the festival of lights celebrated in India. The day is celebrated across India during the Hindu lunisolar month of Kartika. One of the most popular festivals of India, it symbolizes the 'spiritual victory of light over darkness', 'good over evil' and 'knowledge over ignorance'.

Over a period of centuries, Deepavali also saw the use of crackers and light emitting materials during the celebration of this festival. The light and sound producing materials are manufactured using chemicals and metals in different proportions. Technically, this is a class of pyrotechnic devices used for aesthetic and entertainment purposes. The most common use of fireworks is as part of a fireworks display.

Fireworks take many forms to produce the four primary effects of noise, light, smoke, and floating materials (confetti, for example). They may be designed to burn with coloured flames and sparks including red, orange, yellow, green, blue, purple and silver. Displays are common throughout the world and are the focal point of many cultural and religious celebrations.

Depending upon the chemicals used, the crackers produce dust, fine particulate matter, and oxides of carbon, sulphur and nitrogen as well as oxides of various heavy metals. All these cause air pollution, along with noise pollution and health hazards. The problem gets aggravated in bigger cities where there is a high concentration of population, vehicles and industries. Gradually, the festival has turned into a difficult situation. Both the government and the citizenry want a substitute to these pollution generating crackers. So, the challenge is to find an environment-friendly cracker.

In 2016-2017, the Supreme Court of India had directed to the CSIR (Council of Scientific and Industrial Research) laboratories to develop an environment-friendly cracker. The terminology used is 'green fireworks'.

Is it possible to manufacture green fireworks? The answer to the question is 'yes'. It is possible to develop a chemical formulation and standard operating procedures to manufacture green fireworks.

The CSIR laboratories and the R&D department of the Fireworks Association worked in this area. In the year 2019, green firecrackers were sold in the market. The product was developed through design thinking.

In fact, one of the authors Manoj Kumar Patel of the present book has succeeded in making formulations and their theoretical models to establish the eco-friendliness of the crackers. The scope of this book does not permit the author to reveal the sensitive information here. However, it is surely satisfying to mention here that design thinking helped in developing green fireworks.

The celebration of the festival of lights or Deepavali will gradually, over the coming years, become eco-friendly.

3. Productivity Improvement

Salary and wages are fixed for employees at the time of employment in organizations. Employees are given a rise in salaries and wages in order to help them take care of the cost of living adjustment (cola), which is tentatively at par with inflation and value for money. Apart from this, wage revisions are the rightful demands of employees. Wage revisions are made by bipartite discussions between the employee representatives (unions) and management representatives. A third party like the Labour Commissionerate sometimes presides over if the parties in the talks lock horns. Wage revisions are always based on the principle of give and. In a business, rise in wage is possible only when improvement in productivity is achieved. Productivity improvement is possible with the combination of many factors, such as:

a. increase in individual output from employees,
b. increase in production per unit hour or per shift operations,
c. availability of input materials,
d. work and motion studies,
e. machine efficiencies,
f. ergonomics,
g. work environment,
h. clear-cut instructions in the form of specifications and standard operating procedures,
i. adequate skilled manpower, and
j. management support.

The manufacturing organization SMN was doing badly in the market. Its products were not well accepted by the customers (B2B or B2C). Individual productivity and unit productivity were less compared to the industry standards. Work motion studies were carried out about 10 years ago when the Indian economy was protective (not a free market). Workmen were not trained for years. They were not aware of the quality of products produced by them. The business as such was making losses. The owners decided to shut down the business in the next three years. A new CEO was appointed to carry out the processes of plant shutdown. The CEO took charge, made his own assessment, and did something very different. The results were contrary to what he was expected to deliver. Read on.

He called for the first meeting of all the heads of various departments. The purpose of his presence was spelt out by him. The owners' intention to close down the factory was communicated to everyone. He asked for suggestions, if any, from each one present. The first meeting was closed, and it was decided that they would meet again the next day. The observations from the heads of the departments in the next meeting were summarized as follows:

- The balance sheets of the organization were never shared with the heads of the departments by the apex management.
- No heads were aware that their unit was making loss.
- No discussions had been made with them by the corporate finance department or the apex management of the company.
- Capital proposals had been approved by the CFD and MD for the unit even for that year. So, the heads were not aware of the financial crunch their unit was going through.
- There was a feeling that marketing and sales managers were unable to meet their sales targets and hence they were shifting the blame on poor product quality, instead of admitting their own inefficiencies.
- The blame game between the manufacturing and the marketing departments was at its peak.
- Employees on the shop floor and those working on the machines were totally unaware of the status of the company with respect to product quality and poor sales.
- Most of the heads of the departments expressed that they were willing to do whatever was needed to overcome the crisis.
- An agenda was prepared under the leadership of the CEO (who had been given charge to close the factory) to revive the unit from losses to a breakeven level within 18 months.
- The role of the CEO had reversed at the site. Now he had taken the challenge to revive the unit that the owners wanted to close.

The war for survival had begun. But it was easier said than done.

A lot of factors were conceptualized, risks were taken, plans were implemented, and strategies were made. It was a case study in the corporate world that depicted a turnaround of a loss-making company to a profit-making organization. The organization was loss-making in 2001 and, by the end of the year 2003, it had reached its breakeven point. Today, in the year 2020, it is a good profit-making organization. Many of the steps and actions taken were unusual and unthinkable during 2001 when unionism was continuing to be strong in India. This was possible due to the instances of strategy and actions that originated from design thinking. We shall consider the wage negotiations aspect here.

Productivity of CRM 1 was 8 tonnes per shift. That means the output was 1 tonne per hour. The actual output from CRM 1 could become 16 tonnes per shift. Small modifications in the machine and one of the input materials would facilitate production and productivity. The entire operation was semi-automatic. So, higher production did mean higher human effort. The employees were not ready for it. The normal practice in this industry was to give an increase of about 5-6 % and take a salary rise of 10% over and above the cola. It was nearly impossible to drive logic into the minds of the employees to improve production by 100%. The management devised a plan. It was worked out that if an additional mixing process was added and a faster hydrating input was introduced, then the production time per batch would reduce by 40%. The cost of investment was calculated, and it was found that the payback period was 8 months. The sales turnover would double and the fixed costs would reduce by about 25%, even after giving a salary rise of 20% to the workmen. The proposal was discussed well among the heads of production, quality, sales and marketing. The support of everyone was assured. Then the management put forth the proposal to the union representatives. They could not believe that the management had offered them 10% more than their demand. The proposal was accepted and implemented. It was not necessary to bring down the discussion to the employees level. They started giving the desired production of 16-18 tonnes per shift. Thus, they earned an additional incentive for the extra quantity manufactured in their shifts, beyond 16 tonnes.

The problem was debottlenecked and the workmen were happy to give double the production.

That is the beauty of design thinking.

Note: *The detailed calculations are available and anyone interested in the nitty gritty may write to the author of the book.*

4. Duty Is Worship

Let me tell it now!

Honesty often pains; design thinking can ease the pain.

Let Me Tell It Now by Rakesh Maria is worth reading. Rakesh Maria retired from his IPS career as Commissioner of Police, Mumbai. Under his leadership, high profile and sensitive cases like the 1983 Mumbai serial blast and the 19/11 terrorists attack on Mumbai were detected. The duty history of Maria is a testimony to his extreme hard work, dedication and honesty to safeguard the country, even at the expense of his personal responsibilities towards his own family. It is a different matter that each one in his family understood the need of Maria for the country more than themselves.

One of the cases he worked and detected on was related to the 26/11 Mumbai terrorist attack of 2008 in which ACP Ashok Kamte was killed by terrorists on the first day of the attack. Kamte was working under Maria. Vinita, Kamte's wife, cast an aspersion on Maria—that her husband was killed by the bullets fired by the terrorists because of the unwise directives given by Maria during the operation. The pain of losing a loving colleague and the blame from the wife of the deceased was too much for Maria to handle.

One of the other cases unearthed by him was the INX media case involving Indrani Mukerjea and Peter Mukerjea, which revolved around the detection of the murder of Sheena Bora.

Maria has described in his book the torment and mental agony he went through because of the enthusiasm shown by him to solve the above mentioned case. Many fingers were raised about his intent and honesty. Maria suffered a lot mentally. The latter part of the book is replete with descriptions of various incidents, the messages and communications he had made with many people in positions of authority to clarify his good intent, and the fast processing of the said high profile case.

Thinking can be good. Intents can be the best. But there are many people in society who misconstrue good deeds and best intents. The takeaway from the above two cases is that it is prudent to think of the possible adverse consequences of our acts, as people with evil minds and lesser intellects take pleasure in serving good deeds in a bad manner.

Think you should definitely, but do design thinking, because as humans we all get disturbed when our noble acts are painted black.

Suggestion: Read these two good books *Let Me Say It Now* by Rakesh Maria (Westland Publications) and *Mind Without Fear* by Rajat Gupta.

5. After 70 Years

Augmentation for transformation

"In the 21st century, success for individuals, firms, governments and even nations will be defined by the ability to create and innovate," rightly said Amitabh Kant, CEO, NITI Aayog, in the foreword to the book *Modi and Markets* authored by Dhiraj Nayar.

Seventy years after independence, after several steps forward, and perhaps a few backwards, India is finally on the threshold of taking a giant leap towards achieving its unrealized but potential success. Thinking on the areas initiated by private entrepreneurs and industrialists such as Jamshedji Tata, Lovji Nusserwanjee Wadia, Ghansyam Das Birla, Lala Shri Ram, Purushottamdas Thakurdas, Ardeshir Godrej, T V Sundaram Iyengar, Sorabji Pochkhanawala, and Jamnalal Bajaj led to the prospering of businesses and industries. But sectors in the hands of the government did not do well. These sectors were health, education, nutrition and world-class infrastructure. The government could not do as much as the private entrepreneurs could do in their fields.

For the first time, because of the change in thinking and the will in implementation, i.e. by design thinking, India has made a quantum jump to the 42nd position in the ranking system of World Bank in 'ease of doing business'. There has been a radical liberalization in the rules governing foreign direct investment (FDI) across an entire gamut of sectors. India is now proudly importing defence and ammunition equipment, and medicines from developed countries.

Design thinking and maverick, out-of-the-box thinking boosted India's confidence and developed self-respect in Indian citizens.

Prime Minister Modi has adopted the power of technology and harnessed the principle of competition, usually associated with the private sector, to reinvent governance. For the first time in India's post-independence history, there is an intensive monitoring of flagship government-run programmes. The prime minister took the lead with Pragati video conferencing with secretaries and chief secretaries to find solutions for projects that were either stalled or delayed indefinitely. Through 25 meetings via video conferencing, Narendra Modi succeeded in clearing 227 projects worth more than Rs 10.5

lakh crore. During the wild spread of the Covid-19 pandemic, where people in the developed countries like the U.S., the U.K. and all the European countries have been affected in millions and have died in thousands, the design thinking of Prime Minister Narendra Modi has saved the people of India to a large extent. The power of design thinking is enormous.

The industrialist behind India's first national economic plan; Amal Sanyal;   https://qz.com/india/1464869/the-story-of-jrd-tata-gd-birlas-bombay-plan-for-india/

Modi and Markets – Augments for Transformation; Dhiraj Nayar; Westland Books; 2018.

6. Cotton Stripping Machine

Rural entrepreneur

A farmer, Mansukhbhai Patel, invented a cotton stripping machine that significantly cut the cost of cotton farming and revolutionized India's cotton industry. Patel, who studied till class ten, invented this cotton stripping machine in 1991. Patel's machine helps in removing cotton from semi-opened and unopened shells of various cotton varieties. The machine has won a United States patent.

7. Geospatial Technology

Retail marketing

Grant Hamm and Arick Morton, two Raleigh, North Carolina-based serial entrepreneurs have teamed up to tackle the $1-trillion healthcare real estate market with their latest start-up, VisionLTC. The company is a geospatial market analytics platform for the senior housing, medical office, and healthcare industries. VisionLTC's platform provides operators, owners, investors, lenders, developers and other industry stakeholders with critical market analytics to facilitate improved strategic decision-making. The same powerful tool application of geospatial technology plays a key role in integrated management and applying design thinking in marketing to make businesses a success.

medium.com/@innovatorsprogram

8. Business Resumption

MSIL

Necessity is the mother of invention. Inventions necessarily pass through PDCA and design thinking, consciously or subconsciously. The pandemic due to the Covid-19 virus has paralyzed the entire world. Business and manufacturing have come to a grinding halt.

The essence of design thinking appears ripe at this challenging time in many corners. Car manufacturer Maruti Suzuki India Limited (MSIL) came up with a brilliant way of delivering cars to prospective customers through dealers. It is a good example of design thinking to resume a stalled business.

MSIL announced in the first week of May 2020, i.e. just after the second lockdown period in India, that it has put in place a substantial standard operating procedure (SOP) for its dealer network across the nation. The largest carmaker in the country said this was to ensure a high level of sanitization and hygiene across its dealerships for the safety of employees and customers.

In line with state government guidelines and SOP, MSIL commenced opening its dealerships and delivering its cars to customers who had endured a long waiting period. With safety at the forefront, MSIL labelled these procedures as the new way of life or the 'new normal'.

Kenichi Ayukawa, Managing Director and CEO of MSIL said that customer satisfaction and safety were the top priorities of the brand and all its dealerships were endeavouring to ensure "*complete safety, hygiene and sanitization of all touch points.*" The company intends to ensure a safe buying experience for customers coming in to buy Maruti Suzuki cars. Along with implementing SOP across dealerships, the Indo-Japanese manufacturer has also deployed safety protocols at its manufacturing facilities and service workshops with high-level sanitization procedures, adhering to the government recommendations. The SOP had been designed with all the facets of customer interaction in mind.

A team of experts had studied all the processes involved—from the moment the customer walks into the showroom till the final delivery—before coming up with the solutions for the SOP, according to Maruti

Suzuki. Additionally, buyers can choose their desired vehicle as well as accessories digitally through the Arena and Nexa websites, which offer different personalization options.

Moreover, the dealerships will take care of the complete sterilization of the test drive vehicles before assigning them to the customers for their driving experience. One individual will be allowed to take the test drive with the relationship manager sitting in the back row of seats. The brand also offers door delivery of its cars, and the staff visiting the customer's house would follow all safety protocols.

Surendhar M in Cars NewsMaruti Suzuki on May 6, 2020, 11:31 am; https://gaadiwaadi.com/maruti-suzuki-starts-new-car-deliveries-across-india-following-sop-protocols/amp/

9. Thanos

Agritech drone start-up

Thanos is an agritech drone tech start-up founded by Pradeep Palelli and Prathyush Akepati in 2016. The start-up uses drones to offer innovative solutions to conventional problems. It has been constructing drones as an effective pesticide-spraying technology. The start-up won the Drone Olympics Challenge held in Karnataka, jointly organized by the Ministry of Defence and the Drone Federation of India. Currently, the start-up is working on producing aerial pesticide drones to help farmers in agriculture. This is supported and mentored by a Government of Telangana initiative known as Research and Innovation Circle of Hyderabad (RICH).

10. SatSure

Modern technologies in agriculture

SatSure is an innovative large area analytics start-up, which leverages advances in satellites, machine learning, and big data analytics to provide answers to large area questions across multiple domains such as agriculture, forestry, insurance, irrigation, cities, environment, and oil and gas. The Government of Andhra Pradesh, insurance companies, and other large banks are leveraging the solutions of this start-up. NITI Aayog supported the start-up through initiatives such as the Grand Agriculture Challenge. The SatSure platform enables combining of satellite imagery with weather, IoT, social and economic datasets, among many others, to generate timely, location-specific insights.

Conclusion

It would be unfair on the part of the authors as well as the readers for the last chapter on design thinking to be named 'conclusion'.

Truly, it has so happened that, while we were penning down this chapter, we felt we would cover many things, but we are concluding this book by keeping the facts and innovations on top of the mind. We shall move faster and make this a continuous process. Yes, we will update our first book on the subject of design thinking by bringing in more practical areas related to medicine, biotechnology, food science and diet, heavy machinery like drag lines and shovels, transportation systems, and social innovations.

We hope that this edition of our book will be useful to all groups such as; of students, general people from society, researchers, homemakers, teachers, and industry professionals. It would be an honour to receive feedback from each one of you. Your feedback will help us improve the quality and content of the book in the subsequent editions.

Our efforts would get rewarded when the reader takes up the last part of the book and helps us in solving this real-life problem.

The DDCS organization is a pioneer in the manufacturing field. It has manufactured many products for the last 70 years. Once upon a time, it was the only manufacturer of these products. However, after liberalization of the economy, about 30 more manufacturers came into existence. They all started manufacturing the same products that DDCS was making. The newer companies initially poached skilled managers and workers from DDCS and also copied its manufacturing process. They procured materials from the sources where DDCS was procuring. Over a short period of five years, DDCS started losing its market share. Other companies gained market share.

But DDCS has, over the years, developed good infrastructure. It has powerful systems and resources such as a good technical library, management system, specification sheets, standard operating procedures, quality assurance laboratories, and research and development facilities. Input materials, in-process materials, and finished products get tested with respect to quality parameters as per systems and procedures. Many of the other companies producing similar lines of products do not have in place a good library, systems and procedures, quality, and research and development departments. The intellectual capital and qualifications of the managers of DDCS are superior when compared to that of the other companies. Despite these contrasting points, the products and services of DDCS have been found to be of lower quality compared to the products of the newer companies.

Now, the management of DDCS is almost running its last leg in the race of business.

Could you jot down these, please?

- *The inputs you would need to solve this difficult situation of DDCS*
- *A strategy that will relieve DDCS from its present abeyance*
- *Any design thinking idea.*

References

Abbaspour H., Drebenstedt C., Badroddin M., Maghaminik A.; Optimized design of drilling and blasting operations in open pit mines under technical and economic uncertainties by system dynamic modelling; International Journal of Mining Science and Technology; Volume 28, Issue 6, November 2018, Pages 839-848; https://www.sciencedirect.com/science/article/pii/S2095268616302695

Bailin, S., Case, R., Coombs, J., & L. Daniels. (1999). Conceptualizing critical thinking. Journal of Curriculum Studies, 31(3):285-302.

Blank, S. G., & Dorf, B. (2012). The startup owner's manual. the step-by-step guide for building a great company. Pescadero, Calif.: K&S Ranch, Inc.

Boratav, K. (1988). Türkiye İktisat Tarihi 1908-1985. İstanbul: Gerçek Yayınevi. Brown, T. (2008). Design thinking. Harvard Business Review (6), 84.

Burden, R. (1998). Assessing children's perceptions of themselves as learners and problem-solvers: The construction of the myself-as-a-learner scale (MALS). School Psychology International, 19(4), 291-305.

Burnette, C. (2005). IDESIGN: Seven Ways of Design Thinking, A teaching resource. Retrieved from http://www.idesignthinking.com/main.html.

Carroll, M., Goldman, S., Britos, L., Koh, J., Royalty, A. & Hornstein, M. (2010). Destination, imagination and the fires within: Design thinking in a middle school classroom. International Journal of Art and Design Education, 29(1), 37-53. Retrieved from http://www.stanford.edu/

dept/SUSE/takingdesign/proposals/Destination_Imagination_the_ Fire_Within.pdf.

Cowperthwaite M., Zwisler W.H., Tiger computer program documentation, Stanford Research Institute, Publication No. Z106, 1973.

Davis, M. (1998). Making a case for design-based learning. Arts Education Policy Review, 100(2), 7-14.

Dewey, J. (1910). How we think. Boston: Heath.

Dow, P. (2012). An experience of "yes": Independent schools begin to explore and exploit the power of design thinking. Independent Schools Magazine, Spring 2012. Retrieved from http://www.nais.org/ Magazines-Newsletters/ISMagazine/Pages/An-Experience-of-Yes. aspx.

Drucker, P. (1985). The Discipline of Innovation. Harvard Business Review, 63(3), 67–72.

Glen, R., Suciu, C., C., & Anson, R. (2015). Teaching Design Thinking in Business Schools. The International Journal of Management Education, 13, 182–192.

Grace, Chart, M, 2006 laboratory manual of the soil microbial biomass group.

Harald, F.O et al, Potentials of entrepreneurial design thinking for entrepreneurship education, 4th International conference on New Horizons in Education; Procedia – Social and Behavioral Sciences 106 (2013) 2080 – 2092.

Hoffman, R., & Casnocha, B. (2012). The start-up of you. New York, NY: Crown Business.

Hokanson, B. (2007). By measure: Creativity in design. Paper presented at Conference: Creativity or Conformity? Building Cultures of Creativity in Higher Education, University of Wales Institute, Cardiff, Wales, UK.

Ingalls Vanada, D. (2013). Developing dynamic artist/teacher/leaders in preservice art education programs. In D. Flinders & P.B. Uhrmacher (Eds.), Curriculum and Teaching Dialogue, Volume 15 (pp. 101–116). Charlotte, NC: Information Age Publishing.

Iyenger, S.R, Bhav, 2005 composting of house hold waste.

Jeanne Liedtka; Why design thinking works; September–October 2018 Issue; https://hbr.org/2018/09/why-design-thinking-works

Johansson-Sköldberg, U., Woodilla, J., & Çetinkaya, M. (2013). Design Thinking: Past, Present and Possible Futures. Creativity & Innovation Management, 22(2), 121-146, doi:10.1111/caim.12023.

Kelley, T., & Littman, J. (2005). The ten faces of innovation: IDEO's strategies for beating the devil's advocate & driving creativity throughout your organization. New York, NY: Currency/Doubleday.

Kumar, V. (2013). 101 design methods: a structured approach for driving innovation in your organization.Hoboken, N.J.: Wiley.

Marshall, J. (2005). Connecting art, learning and creativity: A case for curriculum integration. Studies in Art Education, 46(3), 227-241.

Mishra A. K., Sen A., Sain D.; Innovative developments in drilling and blasting techniques for rapid excavation of drivages in mines; Journal of Mines, Metals and Fuels 61(7):194-201 · July 2013; https://www.researchgate.net/publication/289304628_Innovative_developments_in_drilling_and_blasting_techniques_for_rapid_excavation_of_drivages_in_mines

Melles, G., Howard, Z., & Thompson-Whiteside, S. (2012). Teaching Design Thinking: Expanding Horizons in Design Education. Procedia – Social and Behavioral Sciences, 31, 162-166,

doi:10.1016/j.sbspro.2011.12.035.

Michalko, M. (2006). Thinkertoys: a handbook of creative-thinking techniques. Berkeley, Calif.: Ten Speed Press.

Moustapha Kebe, Recent Advancement in drilling and blasting; Conference Paper; Recent Technology Advancement in Mining, Bangalore; May 2019; https://www.researchgate.net/publication/333448464_RECENT_ADVANCEMENT_IN_DRILLING_AND_BLASTING

Müller, R. M., & Thoring, K. (2012). Design thinking vs. lean startup: A comparison of two user-driven innovation strategies.

Nikhil Chandwani; The importance of the Gurukul system and why Indian education needs it; https://timesofindia.indiatimes.com/blogs/desires-of-a-modern-indian/the-importance-of-the-gurukul-system-and-why-indian-education-needs-it/

Ozan Soyupak, Humanur Bagli; Design Thinking as a Catalyst for Technology Start-Ups; Research in Business and Social Science; IJRBS Vol 8 No 4, ISSN: 2147-4478; https://doi.org/10.20525/ijrbs.v8i4.289

Papliński A., Equilibrium thermochemical calculations for a great mount of components (in Polish), Biul. WAT, 1993, 42(11), 123-143.

Razzouk, R. & Shute, V. (2012). What is design thinking and why is it important? Review of Educational Research, 82(3), 330-348.

Rikke Friis Dam and Yu Siang Teo; 5 stages in Design Thinking Process; https://www.interaction-design.org/literature/article/5-stages-in-the-design-thinking-process

Essay on Green Revolution in India; Rucha Kanolkar; http://www.economicsdiscussion.net/essays/green-revolution-essays/essay-on-green-revolution-in-india/17559

Ruscic B., Uncertainty Quantification in Thermochemistry, Benchmarking Electronic Structure Computations, and Active Thermochemical Tables. Int. J. Quantum Chem. 114, 1097-1101 (2014).

Seenarious. Lawes, R.A 2009 integrating effects of climate and plant available soil water holding capacity. Volume 113, Issue 3, Pages 297–305.

Singh S. P.; New trends in drilling and blasting technology; International Journal of Surface Mining, Reclamation and Environment; Volume 14, Issue 4, 2000; https://www.tandfonline.com/doi/abs/10.1080/13895260008953338?journalCode=nsme19

Stephen J. Klippenstein, Lawrence B. Harding, and Branko Ruscic, Chemical Sciences and Engineering Division, Argonne National Laboratory, Argonne, Illinois 60439, United States, J. Phys. Chem. Ab Initio Computations and Active Thermochemical Tables Hand in Hand: Heats of Formation of Core Combustion Species, A, 2017, 121 (35), pp 6580–6602, DOI: 10.1021/acs.jpca.7b05945, Publication Date (Web): July 31, 2017.

Sternberg, R. (2008). Increasing academic excellence and enhancing diversity are compatible goals. Educational Policy, 22(4), 487-514.

Sternberg, R., & Grigorenko, E. (2004). Successful intelligence in the classroom. Theory into Practice, 43(4), 274-280.

Sternberg, R., & the Rainbow Project Collaborators (2006). The rainbow project: Enhancing the SAT through assessments of analytical, practical, and creative skills. Intelligence, 34(4), 321-350.

Sujatha K. N. et al. Assessment of Soil Properties to Improve Water Holding Capacity in Soils International Research Journal of Engineering and

Technology (IRJET) e-ISSN: 2395 – 0056 Volume: 03 Issue: 03 | Mar-2016.

Tad Simons, Arvind Gupta and Mary Buchanan; Innovation in R&D: Using design thinking to develop new models of inventiveness productivity and collaboration; https://link.springer.com/article/10.1057/jcb.2011.25

Uzoma, K. C.; Inoue, M.; Andry, H.; Zahoor, A.; Nishihara, E. Influence of biochar application on sandy soil hydraulic properties and nutrient retention. J. Food Agric. Environ. 2011, 9, 1137–1143.

Vygotsky, L. (1978). Mind in society: The development of higher psychological processes. Cambridge, MA: Harvard University Press.

Whitaker, J.; McNamara, N. P.; Reay, D. S. The effect of biochar addition on N2O and CO2 emissions from a sandy loam soil. The role of soil aeration. Soil Biol. Biochem. 2012, 51, 125–134. Case, S. D.; The power of design thinking; https://www.mckinsey.com/business-functions/mckinsey-digital/our-insights/the-power-of-design-thinking

http://stemlock.com/products/stemplug/

http://www.oresomeproducts.com/wp-content/uploads/2013/10/Vari-Stem-business-case-September-2013-Oresome-Products-AUS.pdf Stemplug blasting application at EGAT-Mae Moh Lignite Mine: On-the-field Testing P. Bunnaul1*, J. Dumrongrit2, K. Santawong1, W. Lheewijit3 and V. Rachpech1 1Department of Mining and Materials Engineering, Faculty of Engineering, Prince of Songkla University, Songkhla, Thailand 2 Rajamangala University of Technology Lanna, Chiangmai, Thailand 3 Electricity Generating Authority of Thailand, Lampang, Thailand * Author to correspondence: pitsanu.b@psu.ac.th

https://www.quora.com/Who-started-the-Green-Revolution-in-India   A critical review of the green revolution in India; Agriculture, Policy, 22 May 2018; https://www.geographyandyou.com/a-critical-review-of-the-green-revolution-in-india/ Meaning and Impact of the green revolution in India; https://www.jagranjosh.com/general-knowledge/the-green-revolution-1448273209-1

https://www.livemint.com/news/india/fci-s-surplus-rice-stocks-to-be-converted-into-ethanol-to-make-hand-sanitisers-11587408039897.html Centre permits conversion of surplus rice to ethanol for hand sanitizers;   https://www.business-standard.com/article/economy-policy/centre-permits-conversion-of-surplus-rice-to-ethanol-for-hand-sanitisers-120042001529_1.html

https://knoema.com/aulvzxc/district-wise-rainfall-data-for-india

https://data.gov.in/resources/rainfall-central-india-10-subdivision-and-its-departure-normal-monsoon-session-june-sept

https://www.lowyinstitute.org/the-interpreter/india-s-latest-crisis-600-million-people-struggle-drought

https://niti.gov.in/writereaddata/files/document_publication/2018-05-18-Water-index-Report_vS6B.pdf 2011 Census of India Planning Commission Databook 2014; India Energy Statistics 2015

https://www.irjet.net/archives/V3/i3/IRJET-V3I3373.pdf

https://www.birac.nic.in/desc_new.php?id=89

https://www.financialexpress.com/economy/privatisation-enters-agri-market-for-the-first-time-farmers-will-have-option-other-than-govt/1945836/ Plaster, E. J. 1996. Soil Science and Management. 3rd ed. Albany: Delmar Publishers,

https://m-economictimes-com.cdn.ampproject.org/c/s/m.economictimes.com/news/economy/agriculture/200-more-mandis-added-to-enam/amp_articleshow/75497843.cms; 200 more mandis added to eNAM.